"*The Gift of Loss* is a thoroughly insightful guide written on behalf of infants and children—a straightforward, healthy approach to parenting that will provide children with the security, self-esteem, and self-awareness they need to cope with life's disappointments and losses. A needed alternative to less emotionally engaged parenting styles, this book encourages parents to create a relationship of trust and safety by responding to their children when they yearn to be held, touched, and nurtured. When these children become adults, they will experience loss as a normal part of life from which they can heal because they have learned 'good grieving.' I recommend this lovely work to all parents, caregivers, and those teaching parenting classes."

JANE LINDBERG, LCSW
DIRECTOR OF PSYCHOSOCIAL SERVICES/GRIEF THERAPIST
HINDS HOSPICE, FRESNO

"It gives me great joy to recommend *The Gift of Loss.* In this meaningful and wonderfully practical presentation, my former student, Grace Davis, brings basic child development principles to life through real-life examples and the use of cogent, poignant quotations. Only when readers go through this anguish themselves will they truly understand the value of this book. My own son recently died of cancer, leaving his young widow and eighteen-month-old daughter, Anna. Anna's mother and I have spent hours pondering the exact questions this book addresses. It is remarkable to realize that a former student has given me the guidance I need, and I thank Grace for reassuring me through these pages that we are doing the right thing for little Anna. It is a privilege to publicly praise Grace for her excellent accomplishment."

DORIS O. SMITH, EdD
EARLY CHILDHOOD EDUCATION PROGRAM COORDINATOR
CALIFORNIA STATE UNIVERSITY, FRESNO (RETIRED)

"I am happy to endorse *The Gift of Loss*. This book deals factually with the stages of child development and teaches parents how to deal with losses in a loving manner and with common sense. The discussion on attachment is particularly timely and well presented. A great 'how to' book!"

LURA J. REDDINGTON, MD
OBSTETRICS AND GYNECOLOGY

The GIFT *of* LOSS

How to Raise Emotionally Resilient Children from Birth through Five Years

GRACE E. DAVIS
with Judith St. Pierre, PhD

ABIDING BOOKS

THE GIFT OF LOSS
published by Abiding Books

International Standard Book Number: 0-9744284-5-0

Cover photo and design by Crown Marketing and Design
Interior design by Pamela McGrew

Printed in the United States of America

For information:
ABIDING BOOKS • P.O. BOX 243 • CONDON, OR 97823

Library of Congress Cataloging-in-Publication Data

Davis, Grace E.
The gift of loss : how to raise emotionally resilient children / by Grace E. Davis with Judith St. Pierre.
p. cm.
Includes bibliographical references.
ISBN 0-9744284-5-0 (pbk. : alk. paper)
1. Resilience (Personality trait) in children. 2. Loss (Psychology) in children. 3. Child rearing. I. St. Pierre, Judith. II. Title.
BF723.R46D38 2004
649'.7—dc22
2004003991

04 05 06 07 08 09 10—10 9 8 7 6 5 4 3 2 1 0

To my parents:
Mr. and Mrs. James E. Booze

And to my children, their spouses, and my grandchildren:
Jim and Linda Davis, Kim and David Grimm,
Kristin, Caitlin, Jessica, and Stephanie.

Contents

Preface

The impetus for this book occurred many years before I recognized its import to my understanding of human development, my own life, or my life's work. While I was attending nursing school, my younger brother, Raymond, was killed in an accident on our family farm. He was thirteen years old.

During the first months after his death, my five-year-old sister would dream that he was sitting at the foot of her bed with a halo around his head, talking with her. She would tell us what they talked about. We could see that her dreams were very real to her, and we knew they disturbed her, but we didn't know how to respond. We didn't know how important it was to talk about our loss and grief, and there was no one who could help us understand our feelings.

The second catalyst for this book was my experience working as part of a team in a special education program for the disabled. Some of our students died, and at their funerals I saw how their families' losses had made them strong. They understood the value of faith, of sharing with and supporting one another, and of rebonding through the expression and validation of all the feelings that accompany grief. It was from them that I learned good grieving.

When, more than forty years later, my family finally began to talk about Raymond's accident, I was struck by their vivid recollections of his death, the guilt and sorrow they still felt, and the hurt that remained unhealed. Not knowing how to accept and work through their grief at the time of the accident, they had shut down their feelings and kept silent about it for decades. During our conversation they shed tears of release.

To learn and teach children good grieving is to give them the gift of a lifetime. This book is my celebration of that truth.

Grace E. Davis

Acknowledgments

My heartfelt thanks for the help and encouragement of all the dear people who made up my support group during the writing of *The Gift of Loss* and whose expertise enriched the book:

- Lillian Brown Harrison, PhD, clinical psychologist and consultant, for contributing her knowledge of children and family therapy.
- Sue Ammen, PhD, child psychologist and play therapist, for sharing her expertise in trauma and attachment work with at-risk parents and young children.
- Doris O. Smith, EdD, California State University, Fresno (CSUF), Early Childhood Education Program Coordinator (retired), for her help and encouragement.

- The librarians at Fresno Fig Garden Regional Library for their indefatigable book searches and the Northwest Church Library, Fresno City Schools IMC department, Petunias Children's Store, and Barnes and Noble for their generous help.
- Angelica Carpenter, curator of the Arnie Nixon Children's Library, CSUF, and Jennifer Crow for their gracious help with the children's bibliography.
- Sister Raphael (now deceased), CSC Hospice Director, Saint Agnes Medical Center, Fresno, for encouraging me to write a book about children and loss.
- Robert W. Lindroth (now deceased), *Chicago Tribune*, for his stories and expertise.
- Sylvia and Jim Robbins for their valuable input about the lives of preschoolers.
- Jane Lindberg, Psychosocial Services Director and Grief Therapist for Adults and Children, Hinds Hospice, Fresno, for providing material for helping children in grief.
- Edith Flutter (now deceased), for encouraging me and editing the stories I wrote on this long journey.
- My husband, Bob, for his patience and help.
- Judith St. Pierre, PhD, God's gift for a lost manuscript.

The Gift of Loss

INTRODUCTION

I had been away from my soul so long,
so late sleeping, but that dove's crying
woke me and made me cry.
Praise to all early-waking grievers!

RUMI

"Buffy all gone...Buffy all gone," sobbed two-and-a-half-year-old Annie. Annie's faithful companion, who had protected her from all the scary things in the night, had gotten lost in the woods on the family's camping trip.

"It's okay," Annie's mother said. "Don't cry, Annie. We'll buy you another teddy bear when we get home."

When she was four and suddenly had to change preschools, Annie sobbed uncontrollably. "You can't make me go!" she screamed.

Her mother tried to calm her. "Hush, now," she said. "Big girls don't get so upset. Everything's going to be all right. You'll like your new class. You'll make new friends. Come on, let's watch your new Disney video."

In both cases, Annie's concerned and caring mother thought she was helping her daughter by distracting her. But the result was not what she intended, for what Annie learned was that denial and distraction were the best ways to handle her feelings of loss and pain. It was not surprising, then, that when her parents later divorced, fourteen-year-old Annie ran away from home, joined a gang of other runaway teens, and started using drugs.

When it comes to grieving, our culture has been away from its soul for a long time. This basic life skill has been at best ignored and at worst considered something shameful. The result has been that we have not taught our children how to cope with the changes and losses that are a part of life, and so when they occur—as they inevitably do—our children are not prepared.

Giving young Annie permission to grieve minor losses and upsetting changes, to feel and express her anger and sadness, could have taught her to manage her grieving instead of running away from it. It could have taught her that pain is bearable. She could have learned how to receive comfort from others and how to comfort herself as she worked through her feelings of loss. But Annie didn't learn that, and when she was faced with the major loss of her parents' divorce, she didn't know how to deal with it. So she ran away and used drugs to ease her emotional pain.

Losses are part of life. Some we can predict; some we can't control. As a parent, you can't prevent your child from experiencing the pain of loss. You can, however, teach him how to cope with it.[1] I call successful coping "good grieving," and in this book I share with you the knowledge and skills you need to help your child grieve three different kinds of loss at three different stages in his development.

Because children experience their world and events in their lives in very different ways as they grow, I talk about early childhood losses for infants (newborn to twelve months), for toddlers (one to three years), and for preschoolers (three to five years). Almost without exception, all children experience separation, weaning, and toilet training. These losses are a normal part of a child's development. Then there are losses that, while not linked to developmental milestones, are common during childhood. These losses include the birth of a sibling, moving, and the death of a pet. Finally, there are major losses like death, divorce, and disasters. These are life-rocking events that can strike anyone at anytime. Preparing your child to cope with them is why learning and practicing good grieving in early childhood is so important—and why the sooner it is begun, the better.

> *And if not now, when?*
>
> THE TALMUD

In the first five years of life, healthy emotional communication is like a dance in which you and your child constantly learn new ways to synchronize your moods and movements. For that reason, I address childhood losses from your perspective as well as your child's. To help your child grieve well, you must take care of yourself, and throughout this book I give you tips to help you do that as well as ways to help him.

The Chinese ideogram for *crisis* combines two characters: One means *calamity*; the other means *opportunity*. The developmental losses that are calamities for your young child can be opportunities for you. By acknowledging his losses, encouraging him to express his pain, and providing the support and structure he needs to cope, you can help him become emotionally resilient—strong enough to live life fully amid the crises that life inevitably brings.

The more opportunities your child has to learn to cope with the little losses of childhood, the better able he will be to gain from all the changes in his life. For children who have learned good grieving, many of life's stressful events become challenging learning experiences on the road to maturity. And when a child learns and grows through grief, small losses lead to big gains. That's when loss becomes a gift.

There is no such thing as a grief that doesn't have a gift in it.

God Answers

I asked God to take away my habit.
God said, "No. It is not for Me to take it away,
but for you to give it up."
I asked God to make my handicapped child whole.
God said, "No. His spirit is whole.
His body is only temporary."
I asked God to grant me patience.
God said, "No. Patience is a by-product of tribulations.
It isn't granted; it is learned."
I asked God to give me happiness.
God said, "No. I give you blessings.
Happiness is up to you."
I asked God to spare me pain.
God said, "No. Suffering draws you apart from worldly cares,
and brings you closer to Me."
I asked God to help my spirit grow.
God said, "No. You must grow on your own.
But I will prune you to make you fruitful."
I asked God for all things that I might enjoy life.
God said, "No. I will give you life,
so that you may enjoy all things."
I asked God to help me love others as much as He loves me.
God said, "Ahhh, finally you have the idea.
To the world you might be one person,
but to one person you just might be the world."

God's no is always a yes.

1

Another Language

If I speak in the tongues of men and of angels, but have not love, I am only a resounding gong or a clanging cymbal.

1 Corinthians 13:1

If we were to take all the loving, caring parents in the country and look at how they communicate about feelings with their children, we would come up with at least four different groups. As you read the following descriptions, think about your own style of communicating with your children, as well as what you learned from your own parents.

When my child is angry or sad or scared:

- I try to ignore it or distract him from his negative feelings.
- I tell him to be quiet, and if his behavior is inappropriate, I tell him there will be consequences if he doesn't stop.
- I tell him I understand how he is feeling and allow him to express his emotions even if his behavior is inappropriate.
- I try to calm him by helping him become aware of, label, and express his feelings, but I also set limits on inappropriate behaviors.

Which group did you identify with? Once you have decided, see which of the following descriptions best describes your motives and feelings:

- I'm good at protecting my child and feel uncomfortable when he experiences negative feelings.
- I'm good at setting limits for my child so he can learn to control his behavior.
- I'm good at allowing my child to express negative feelings, but I'm not always sure how to set limits.
- I'm good at allowing my child to express negative feelings, and I'm comfortable with setting limits.

You might not see yourself in any of these groups. What's important is that you become aware of your communication style and what motivates it. That's because any discussion of children from birth through five years of age necessarily begins with the adults who not only provide for and protect them, but also teach them what they need to know to eventually survive—and thrive—on their own. Self-understanding is essential in learning to communicate emotionally with your child—a kind of communication I call "feeling talk."

Feeling Talk

In a society that values winning, it can be hard to talk about loss and the grieving that accompanies it. Historically, the prescribed response has been to keep a stiff upper lip. Many adults parenting today were raised by parents who didn't know how to cope with negative feelings and so thought that the best way to deal with them was to forget about them and get on with life.

All loving parents want their children to develop the skills they need to live healthy, productive lives, and typically we seize opportunities to help children grow physically and mentally. But we are not so quick to seize—or even recognize—opportunities to help them grow emotionally. One of the reasons for this is that we have long considered certain subjects taboo—among them elimination, sex, and death. Another reason is that we minimize grief experiences. We do not encourage, and sometimes we do not even allow, our children to experience the pain of loss.

It's natural for parents to want to protect their child from pain, including emotional pain. Yet minimizing your child's pain teaches him to avoid or run away from it, and that sets the stage for potentially harmful behaviors later on. The effects of unresolved grief can be seen in truancy, drug use, crime, promiscuity, and even suicide. These and other ills strongly suggest that teaching a child to keep a stiff upper lip is not the way to help him deal with loss and grief. Grieving is a natural healing process, and we now know that the best way to get on with life is to experience our feelings of grief, work through them, and learn and grow from the experience.

Dr. John Gottman recommends that parents and caregivers use the crises in a child's life as opportunities for "emotion coaching." [2] In our competitive society, the word *coaching* often suggests harsh demands to win, but in the vocabulary of feeling talk, coaching means helping a child identify, talk about, and work through the emotions associated with loss. Children who learn to communicate their emotions in a healthy way tend to perform better in school and be more resilient when faced with difficult emotional situations. They get mad and sad and scared when things get tough, but they bounce back and go on more readily than other children. Life's blows hurt but do not devastate them.

Emotion coaching—helping your child learn to control his

impulses, delay gratification, motivate himself, read other people's social cues, and cope with life's ups and downs—requires you to be in touch with your own feelings. A child learns feeling talk from his parents, so if you don't speak it yourself, you can't teach it to him.

Feeling talk is a skill that takes practice to develop. Opportunities to grow emotionally continue throughout our lives, but what we make of them depends a great deal on what happened in our own childhood. By the time we are adults, many of us have decided on some level not to keep growing. At some critical juncture we chose the old over the new because our caregivers did not give us the support we needed in a frightening or painful situation.

As a parent, your beliefs are related to the way you handle your child's feelings. If you believe that expressing sadness is a sign of weakness, that anger is a sign of willfulness, or that fear is a sign of immaturity, even with the best of intentions you will try to avoid or suppress those feelings in yourself and in your child. But if you believe that it's not only okay, but actually healthy to express negative feelings, you're more likely to use the situations that evoke them as opportunities to coach your child through them.

Let's look at how you can develop healthy emotional communication skills to pass on to your children.

> *When one is out of touch with oneself, one cannot reach others.*
>
> ANN MORROW LINDBERGH

TAKE CARE OF YOURSELF FIRST

Your plane is about to take off, and you're seated next to your three–year-old, listening to the flight attendant give the usual instructions: "In the event that the cabin loses pressure, an oxygen mask will fall from the compartment above you. Slip the mask over your nose and mouth and breathe normally. If you are traveling with children, put on your own mask first and then help them."

How do you react? If you're like most parents, you probably want to help your child first. Yet a child requires less oxygen than you do, and if you pass out from oxygen deprivation, you won't be able to help your child at all. The same is true when you are responding to your child's emotional needs. You need to take care of your own needs before you try to help him.

A case in point...

My five-year-old granddaughter, Julie, sustained severe burns to her legs and back in an accident. I took her to her first physical therapy session and stayed with her during the treatment. The night before we went to the clinic, I didn't sleep well, and I felt vulnerable even before I picked her up. Then when I saw the pain the therapy caused her, my tears began to flow, and I couldn't stop them.

After the treatment, the therapist took me aside and said, "If this is too difficult for you, have someone else bring Julie. She needs to feel supported by the adult who comes with her." When I thought about what had happened, I realized that if I had been well rested, I could have supported Julie instead of becoming overly emotional.

The night before Julie's next treatment, I made sure I got plenty of sleep, and the next morning before I picked her up, I said a little prayer.

This grandmother's situation was especially demanding because Julie's loss was also a loss for her. In such cases, you might not have enough energy or resources to do it all on your own. That's when you need to ask for help.

As you retire to rest, give your soul and God a time together...and deep and profound developments will go on in spirit, soul, and body.

OSWALD CHAMBERS

DEVELOP A SUPPORT SYSTEM

Besides monitoring your own emotional well-being and doing all you can to ensure that your needs are met, you can enhance your ability to care for your child by establishing a reliable support system. Parenting is an awesome responsibility, and all caregivers can use help from time to time. To get it, you must deliberately create support systems by searching for the information that will lead you to people who share your concerns.

In times past, family bonds, neighborhood ties, and sense of community provided people with support in difficult times. But contemporary society is different. Family members are no longer automatically sources of support. Members of a single-family unit may live far away from or be estranged from one another. In this highly mobile and less community-based world, people often do not even know their neighbors. Today, a support system consists of all the people who offer you strength, wisdom, and assistance in coping with a complex world. It can include professionals—

doctors, teachers, counselors, clergy, therapists, and community service providers—as well as your family, friends, neighbors, and perhaps even the members of a support group.

You can tap into many resources besides family, friends, and neighbors. The telephone directory for one city of 350,000 has more than five pages of listings of community services available by phone, including fifty-seven separate groups or organizations whose members are willing and able to help. Services include child care and mother and child health. In some communities a "warm line" is available twenty-four hours a day to address caregivers' problems and concerns. Religious groups offer support services for families and communities. There are many books on the subject, and you can find helpful information in parenting magazines and at sites on the Internet as well.

Finding people who are also raising young children is particularly helpful because it allows you to compare notes. Nothing is quite as reassuring as knowing that others are going through the same thing with their child as you are with yours.

> *A case in point...*
>
> After I had my first baby, I continued to meet once a week with four other mothers from my birthing class. We experienced everything about our first children together—the joys, the challenges, the ups and downs, the trials and tribulations, the good days and bad. We exchanged ideas and suggestions. We socialized with each other and helped one another with child care. That group was my lifeline for three and a half years!

Your child also needs a support group, and its most important member is *you*. He needs your love and support from the moment he is conceived until he reaches adulthood—and often beyond. His mental, physical, emotional, and spiritual health depend upon your support more than on any other thing. You owe it to yourself and him to develop a base of support that will sustain both of you during times of stress, change, and loss.

Listen with Your Heart

Grieving people want and need to be heard. To a great degree, good grieving is about being heard. Some people never express their feelings even in prayer because they have never been allowed to express what they truly feel. Yet prayer and faith are wonderful healing tools.

In explaining why he became a Christian, Tolstoy said it was because he saw that the people around him who had that faith had derived from it an idea of life that gave them strength to live and strength to die in peace and joy. Henry Fosdick wrote that real Christians do not carry their religion; their religion carries them. Instead of weighing them down, their religion lifts them up and carries them over the hard places.[3]

True religion does not impose burdens that are repressive to mind and spirit. Grace, not law, is the heart of its message. When we live by the law, we constantly feel condemned. But when we live by grace, we begin to see God the way He really is—as one who not only loves and accepts us, but also listens and speaks to us. This is the kind of grace your grieving children need from you.

When you are really listening to your child, you look into his eyes to get a glimpse of his soul. You pay attention to his body language as well his words because you know that nonverbal clues such as posture, tone of voice, and facial expression can either contradict or reinforce what he says. This is especially important when you're talking with a young child, for he is only beginning to develop his communication skills and can have difficulty expressing what he is feeling.

If you truly wish to understand what is going on inside a child, listening will require you to pay attention, take your time, and be patient. If he is experiencing grief, you will have to consciously set aside your desire to hurry the healing process. It's important to understand that grief and grieving are different. Grief is the feeling inside him; grieving, or mourning, is the process by which he lets that feeling out. Kids need to mourn so they can start feeling better; if they keep everything inside, they'll just feel worse.[4] As your child's emotion coach, your job is to help him get his feelings out so he can begin to heal.

> *Give sorrow words. The grief that does not speak whispers the o'er-fraught heart and bids it break.*
>
> SHAKESPEARE

Listening with your heart allows you to respond to your child's feelings with empathy. Empathy is the capacity to understand a situation from another's viewpoint and to respond accordingly. It is not the same as sympathy, for while sympathy is based on experiencing the same emotions as another, empathy is not. You have to work hard to understand what another person is feeling when it's different from what you're feeling.

A case in point...

One hot summer my daughter Sandra moved into a new home. Stressed from the move, she immediately came down with a bad case of the flu. After two days, she was so weak that she couldn't take care of her fourteen-month-old daughter, Katy, and so she called me.

"Katy won't leave my side," she said. "Please come help us."

When I arrived, Sandra was on a mattress on the floor by the bathroom, and Katy was next to her, whimpering. Putting my arms around my granddaughter, I whispered, "Mommy's sick. Let's go to your room to play. But as I carried her to her room, Katy began to scream. I sat down in the rocking chair to soothe her, but to no avail.

Finally I stopped to think about how Katy was feeling. She must have seen Sandra vomiting, and that had to have been frightening. She knew something was wrong with her mother, and she didn't want to be away from her. I had been so intent on giving my daughter relief that I hadn't stopped to view the situation from Katy's perspective.

So back to the mattress we went. After a while Sandra fell asleep, and so did Katy.

Once you have achieved an empathic understanding of what your child is feeling in the here and now, you have to convey your understanding to him in such a way that he feels affirmed and secure. Empathic communication helps you build a relationship based on trust. The more your child trusts you to understand and accept his feelings, the easier it will be for him to be open about his feelings and for you to coach him through emotionally trying situations.

Power Points

- ✓ Take care of yourself first.
- ✓ Develop a support system.
- ✓ Listen with your heart.

Taking care of your own emotional needs, developing a support system, and learning to listen with your heart will help you develop the emotional communication skills you need to help coach your child as he moves through the developmental stages of childhood. Try to find as many opportunities as you can to practice feeling talk. As you do, you'll foster in yourself the skills you will eventually teach your child.

> *A good house has strong walls. The space within the walls makes it a home. Create space within your heart and your children will always rest secure.*
>
> William Martin

2

THE TIE THAT BINDS

*This very communicative system that
you and your baby form in your first year—
even in your first weeks together—
that is the prelude to the way you'll
dance together the rest of your lives.*

EVELYN THOMAN

From the moment your baby is born, you begin a "dance" of emotional communication with him. And like any dance, it's awkward at first because you have to win his trust and learn how to communicate your own feelings in a loving and supportive way. With each new stage of your child's development, you both must learn and practice new skills. Creating a secure attachment bond with your baby is the prelude to teaching him to self-soothe, a crucial skill for good grieving.

Your newborn baby wants to trust you. That's because he cannot survive on his own. He needs someone to feed him, change him, hold him, love him, comfort him, play with him, and make him feel safe, and he naturally seeks out a relationship with his parents or caregivers. Over time that relationship can develop into a secure attachment bond.

"Of course!" you say. "But what does that have to do with grieving losses?"

Just this: When your baby feels that secure bond, he knows he's safe, and that makes him more willing to explore not only the world around him, but also the world of feelings inside him. Without the security of an attachment bond, it's very difficult for a young child to handle the emotions associated with loss.

> *Oh, the comfort, the inexpressible comfort of feeling safe with a person.*
>
> DINAH MULOCK CRAIK

HOW A SECURE ATTACHMENT BOND DEVELOPS

When your baby has a secure attachment to you, he feels not only safe, but also intensely loved and content in your presence. Your baby may bond with only one or two special caregivers before he develops relationships with others in the family. On the other hand, if many people in your family are involved in caring for him, he may develop several secure attachment bonds and have something like an "attachment network," or safety net of people with whom he feels safe and comfortable.

It doesn't seem to matter how many secure attachments a baby has; what's important is that he have at least one. Children who lack a secure attachment don't feel as comfortable exploring their physical world or their feelings. That means they might have more problems controlling their emotions and behavior and a harder time getting along with other children.

Your baby doesn't automatically have a secure attachment bond with you. Secure attachment bonds begin at birth, or even before, and continue developing throughout childhood. Regardless of differences in culture and caregiving practices, your baby goes through well-defined phases in developing this secure attachment.

The preattachment phase

During the first few weeks of your baby's life, he will be very interested in the people around him, especially in their faces and voices. He will prefer the human voice to other sounds and may show special recognition of your voice. He will give signals, such as crying, that are likely to bring him attention and care. At about four to six weeks, he will smile at anyone who engages with him. This "social smile" tends to make people want to stay and interact with him more. In this phase, a baby doesn't show strong preferences for any of the people around him, including his parents.

An attachment-in-the-making

During this phase, a baby begins to prefer to interact with familiar people, and that usually means his parents. He shows this by directing his behaviors and signals toward you more than others. It's hard to say exactly when this stage begins, because it develops earlier in smell and touch than it does in hearing or sight. It's an ongoing process that takes place over several months.

At two days old, a baby prefers the smell of his own mother's milk to that of another mother. Even at three or four weeks, he may be soothed more easily by the smell and feel of a parent or familiar caregiver. Later, he begins to respond in different ways to familiar and unfamiliar voices. After four months, his vision is better, and he can recognize people. This means that you get the special smiles. Strangers get fewer, and they may even get frowns. At around five or six months, your baby can reach out for you to let you know he wants you to hold him. You can comfort him more easily than others can. However, if you're not around, he is able to let other people soothe him.

A clear-cut attachment

This phase represents a turning point in your baby's thinking abilities. As his memory develops, he begins to remember you when you aren't around. By this point, his strongest bond is with you, so he protests, often loudly, when you leave him with other people. Although this is a normal, healthy reaction, be prepared for other people to tell you that you have spoiled him.

> *A case in point...*
>
> When Tisha was three months old, my aunt Sally came to help. When Tisha cried and my wife, Sharon, picked her up, Aunt Sally said, "You've just got to stop picking Tisha up every time she cries. You'll spoil her to death!"
>
> Tisha was our first child, and we wanted to do the right thing, so in order not to spoil her, we let her cry for longer and longer periods. But her crying spells just got longer and louder, and she got redder and more out of control every time she cried. Sharon and I were so worried that we finally asked our pediatrician for help. He recommended that we consult a visiting nurse who worked with new parents and their babies.
>
> The nurse happened to arrive in the middle of one of Tisha's crying spells. She immediately picked her up and began to rock her gently and speak softly to her. Soon Tisha began to calm down. Even so, it took twenty minutes for her breathing and heart rate to get back to normal.

This couple learned that they wouldn't spoil their daughter if they picked her up every time she cried. While it's different with older children, crying is the primary way babies tell you what they need. But though that's true, it's also true that not all cries communicate a need for you to respond physically. Waiting is also a response. You don't need to jump up and run into your baby's room the moment he begins to fuss. Let him fuss for a few minutes. However, if he continues to fret or begins to cry, he needs your assistance. His cry is a message to you. Over time he'll develop the ability to be separated from you without protesting. Meanwhile, when he cries, hold him.

> *A case in point...*
>
> When my son Alexi was two days old, I walked down the hall of the hospital to watch him through the nursery window. He was crying. Seeing me looking in, a neonatal nurse came over. "Oh, don't fret about your baby," she said with a laugh. "He just wants to be held."
>
> I thought about this for a split second and then said, "He's two days old. I'll hold him."
>
> As I cradled Alexi, I wondered what possible lesson he could have learned by being left alone to cry.

Partners

This final attachment phase occurs as your child moves into the preschool developmental stage. He's better able to use words to communicate his thoughts and feelings, and he can think ahead.

This means that he can now participate in planning how you and he will grieve a loss. He is becoming a full-fledged partner in the dance. How well he dances will depend to a great extent on how secure his attachment bond is with you.

How to Create Secure Attachment Bonds

There are two things you can do to create a secure attachment bond with your baby.

1. Engage in enjoyable interactions with him.

This doesn't mean that you and your child need to enjoy each other all the time, but it does mean that you need to frequently experience intense pleasure in each other's company. There was a good example of this kind of interaction on a recent episode of *America's Funniest Videos*. Baby is in his high chair, and Daddy is sitting close to him. When Daddy makes eye contact and focuses his full attention on Baby, their dance begins. Baby's eyes are glued to his father's face as Daddy begins to make funny faces. With each one, Baby breaks into peals of laughter. It's clear with each belly laugh that the connection between the father and his child is growing.

2. Respond sensitively to his feelings and needs.

To do this, you have to recognize when your baby is communicating a need and then accurately interpret his communication. Even in the first few minutes and hours of life, babies convey their wishes through facial expressions, gestures, posture, and different kinds of cries. Some babies are better than others at sending signals that are easy to read, and some parents are better than others at reading their baby's signals. Until you learn your baby's language of cries and behavior, of gestures and expressions, you may become frustrated. That's when you should call for help.

A case in point...

I was in a panic. My newborn daughter, Tanya, was my first child. She had been crying hard for fifteen minutes, and nothing I did would quiet her. So I picked up the phone and called Mom.

"Mom, I'm a nervous wreck," I said. "Please come!"

Mom hurried right over. She swaddled Tanya in a baby blanket and then quietly held her against her breast, rocking her and patting her little back. Tanya released a few gas burps from her bottom and quieted right down.

"I don't know why," Mom said, "but babies don't like to let go of gas. I learned that when you were a baby. Holding them this way and patting them helps them release it, and then they're a lot happier."

> *A grandmother is a mother who has a second chance.*

A sensitive response also means responding quickly and consistently to your baby's cues. A baby has a very short attention span, so for him to experience your response as connected to his signal, your reaction must be closely related in time to when he indicated his need. Responding consistently helps him learn to trust that if he lets you know he needs something, most of the time you'll be there to meet the need. Research shows that when parents respond quickly and consistently during the first few months of their baby's life, he will cry less at one year of age than other babies because he will have learned that he can rely on the people in his world to respond to his needs.

Power Points

- ✓ Recognize that your baby signals his needs.
- ✓ Read and interpret his signals accurately.
- ✓ Respond quickly and consistently to his signals.

There will be times when either you or your baby (or both!) will feel angry, frustrated, or exhausted, and you won't be able to respond sensitively. But if you are responsive most of the time, you can create the sense of security he needs to thrive. At those times when you're not, you can come back as soon as you're able to and reconnect emotionally, teaching him by example that when he makes mistakes, he can reach out and reconnect with you. Rocking, cuddling, and holding are particularly good ways to restore your bond.

In recent years, there has been a great deal of interest in the subject of bonding, and as with any topic that draws a lot of attention, myths have grown up around it. These myths can undermine your confidence in yourself as a parent, so to put your mind at ease, let's debunk two of the most common ones.

Myths about Bonding and Attachment

Myth #1: If I don't bond with my baby immediately after birth, he will be perpetually insecure or emotionally handicapped. Bonding with a child begins at different times for different parents. For many mothers and some fathers, it begins when they first find out about the pregnancy. For some it begins with the actual birth; for others it begins even later. While the period right after birth may be the optimal time for bonding to begin, if you and your infant don't experience closeness immediately, your relationship is not doomed.

A case in point...

My first pregnancy ended with a miscarriage at three months. In my second pregnancy, I had medical problems as well, and from the fourth month on I had to be on bed rest. John and I were both so fearful of losing another baby that we couldn't even think about picking out a name.

Our baby boy was born early by cesarean section and was moved to the critical care unit at the children's hospital. John stayed there and began to bond with him, but I still couldn't let myself feel anything for him. It was only when he came home two weeks later and I held him in my arms that I felt an overwhelming rush of love and joy for our son, Justin.

Despite this mother's fear of bonding and her separation from her son after birth, she was eventually able to establish a secure attachment with him. That's because the development of an emotional bond is an ongoing process, not a one-time event. During the first years of your child's life, you and your baby engage in your unique dance, which changes over time.

Myth #2: My baby will have an insecure attachment bond if I don't take all the right steps and do all the right things at the right times.

It is simply impossible to be a sensitive, available, and responsive parent all the time. The latest research shows that among those who love their children and are trying to raise them the best they know how, there are no bad parents. Even more reassuring, it shows that you can best help your baby thrive by relaxing and being yourself instead of worrying about doing everything right. Child expert Evelyn Thoman writes:

> There are as many wonderful ways to raise a baby as there are babies and parents.... You can mess up, and rather than suffering from guilt and possibly disrupting your dance...you can decide, "Hey, I won't do that again," and go on. In a warm, loving, caring family system full of mutual trust and respect, there's plenty of time for both you and your baby.[5]

Missteps are inevitable, but the only real mistake is one from which you learn nothing. Instead of feeling guilty, learn as you keep on dancing. It's the entire dance, not a few missteps, that determines your baby's sense of security.

Power Points

- ✓ Engage in enjoyable interactions with your child.
- ✓ Respond sensitively to his feelings and needs.
- ✓ Relax and be yourself.
- ✓ Learn from your mistakes as you keep on dancing.

Our greatest glory consists not in never falling, but in rising every time we fall.

Ralph Waldo Emerson

3

A Calm Outlook

Hence in a season of calm weather
Though inland far we be,
Our souls have sight of that immortal sea
Which brought us hither.

William Wordsworth

The first five years of life are the critical period for teaching children the basics of emotional communication. When you establish a secure bond with your baby and calm him, you help his brain develop connections between feelings and language, which in turn teach him how to soothe himself, how to control his behavior, and eventually how to view his losses from a larger perspective.

Teaching Your Child to Become Calm

Teaching your child to become calm when he's distressed begins right after birth. You smile at your baby; he smiles back and coos;

you coo back and laugh. Then he turns his head away, signaling his need for less stimulation, and you speak softly to him. He looks back and smiles. He cries; you pick him up and hold him close; he nuzzles into you and fusses. You know he's hungry and you feed him; he calms and looks at you with love as he eats.

As you and your baby engage in this dance, you help him make emotional sense of his experiences. He understands that you know his needs, and he comes to trust that you will meet most of them most of the time. He learns that he can make things happen, that he can let you know he is distressed, and that you will help him feel better.

At first, your baby depends almost totally on you to help him calm when he's distressed. When you allow him to express his feelings in a way that calms him down, you help teach his body what it feels like to be calm. This is called "soothing." After a while, he learns how to calm himself down because he has experienced it with you. This is called "self-soothing." If your baby fusses and then quiets down without your help, you'll know he is learning the art of self-soothing. That's why it's sometimes good to wait a while before you pick him up—you are creating an opportunity for him to learn to self-soothe.

A child who develops this ability is much better at controlling his behavior when he feels negative emotions. You can help him do this by being aware of and respecting his feelings, by helping him structure his emotional experiences, and by staying emotionally grounded yourself.

In quietness and trust is your strength.

ISAIAH 30:15

Be Aware of Your Child's Feelings

To help your child learn to self-soothe, you must be aware of his feelings. Sometimes this is very easy—like when he's howling with rage because he's hungry and his food isn't ready. Other times it's harder to know what he's feeling. As you spend time together developing feeling talk, you'll learn to read his feelings accurately. Here are four things you can do to facilitate this awareness while your child is an infant.

1. Interact with him at feeding time.

Bottle- or breast-feeding your baby is a time of special communication and closeness. If you watch him closely, you'll discover that he seeks out your eyes, reaches for your face or fingers, and communicates nonverbally with you in many ways. When you stroke him gently and talk with him, he senses that you're saying, "You're a wonderful baby. I'm so glad you're here."

A child uses eye contact with his parents (and others) to feed emotionally. The more parents make eye contact with their child as a means of expressing their love, the more the child is nourished with love and the fuller is his emotional tank.

Ross Campbell

2. Massage him.

In *Loving Hands,* Frederick Leboyer describes infant massage as a silent dialogue of love between a parent and baby. This "loving touch" involves not only physically massaging your child, which in itself is nurturing and calming, but also listening to what he wants and likes.[6]

> *A case in point...*
>
> My daughter was born ten days early. The birth was long and difficult, and she started having colic at two weeks of age. I received a gift certificate from a baby massage instructor for massage classes. *Well,* I thought, *Why not try it?*
>
> It was an incredible experience. It helped me learn to be more sensitive to my daughter's nonverbal cues, and I developed a close support system with other mothers in the group. My daughter loved it! Just the sound of my rubbing the oil together in my hands caused her to express delight. It provided a special connecting time for us. And the tummy massage must have helped her colic. After three weeks, it was gone!

3. Wear him.

In many cultures, mothers carry their babies in a front- or backpack while they do their daily chores. Wearing your baby in a pack or sling as you walk, shop, or do the dishes connects you to his feelings and rhythms.

4. Learn his signals.

When your baby is awake, he communicates his needs almost constantly. By observing him carefully, you can learn to differentiate between signals of fear, pain, and anger. Some cries communicate discomforts, like colic; others signify boredom. Still others are your baby's way of letting off steam. With practice you can become expert at understanding your baby's signals. Of course, if you have another baby, you'll need to start over because each child's signals are unique.

As you engage in feeling talk with this little stranger, you'll learn more and more about each other. If you're having difficulty decoding his signals, your pediatrician, family physician, or nurse practitioner may be able to help you or direct you to other resources or helpful individuals. Be sure to consult those who can give you information, not just opinions. Every year we learn more about the way babies grow and develop and how parents and caregivers can sensitively and effectively respond to them. In the bibliography, I've listed some books that can help you understand your baby's body language and signals.

Stay Emotionally Grounded

Ever notice how your child seems to have a bad day on the same day you're having one? If only he could give you a little emotional space! Instead he acts as though he needs you more. He clings, acts out, whines—anything to get your attention. There's actually a good reason for this. You are so important to his sense of safety and comfort that he is very attuned to your emotional state.

This is both a blessing and a curse. If he's distraught or frightened, you can help him by being calm and soothing. But if you're feeling angry, depressed, or anxious—even though your feelings might have nothing to do with him—he is still tuned in to you, and your feelings can add to his distress and create a cycle of escalating emotional intensity.

When your child is in the grip of a strong feeling, particularly if it's difficult or painful, it can be contagious and make you feel out of control as well. It's amazing how someone so small can trigger such powerful feelings of anger and frustration in an adult. To prevent this, you need to understand your own feelings as well as those of your child. Understanding your feelings will greatly facilitate your own self-soothing so you can be emotionally available to him. Self-soothing brings down your heart rate, blood pressure, and respiration so you can listen to what your child says, recognize what he is feeling, and use his emotion as an opportunity for intimacy and teaching. After you have soothed yourself, you can help your child soothe himself.

Once you're aware of your emotions, you'll have to set them aside for the moment so you can respond to your child. This doesn't mean that you shouldn't have these feelings. You might feel angry, frustrated, embarrassed, or helpless. These are natural responses, and at some point you'll need to process them, perhaps with the help of your spouse, a friend, or a counselor. But if you express them toward your child, the situation is likely to spiral downward. Your child needs your help to calm down, and for that you must be emotionally grounded.

By definition, human beings are imperfect, and that includes parents. But even if you lose control of your emotions, it's possible to turn the situation into an opportunity to model emotional responsibility for your child by apologizing instead of blaming your anger on him. And you can model forgiveness for him by forgiving yourself. Children learn the behaviors their parents demonstrate.

By expressing your angry feelings in ways that are not hurtful to your young child, you demonstrate that strong feelings can be expressed and managed. If you refrain from yelling at him when you're angry and instead take time out, pound on a pillow, or go for a walk, you teach him that while all feelings are acceptable, all behaviors are not.

Your children are not your children.... They come through you but not from you, and though they are with you yet they belong not to you.... You are the bows from which your children as living arrows are sent forth.

KAHLIL GIBRAN

Respect Your Child's Feelings

Respecting your child's feelings and boundaries means paying attention to the things that can make him feel fearful or distressed. The key here is to establish good emotional communication—feeling talk—from the very beginning. For instance, when you give your infant a bath, you can tell him, "Now I'm going to turn you on your back and wash your hair." As you wash his hair, track his reactions.

Established early, this practice of talking to your child will help you know how he might respond in other situations involving water, as for example, when you put him in a bathtub or swimming pool for the first time. You will learn how to coach him through new and unfamiliar situations, while he will learn to be calm when he finds himself in them.

Respect also means realizing that your child's emotional reaction may be quite different from what you would like it to be. For instance, demanding that he give you a hug or a kiss is not respecting his feelings.

Children are great imitators, and if your child sees you demonstrating loving behavior, he will most likely give you lots of hugs and kisses. But if he doesn't want to, don't force him. Let him express his feelings sincerely.

A case in point...

When my daughter, Bonnie, was four, my husband's brother came to visit. He was six feet five inches tall and had a deep, booming voice. When Bonnie wouldn't go to him, he exclaimed in a joking kind of way, "Come give your Uncle Rick a kiss or I'll chew your ears off!"

So much for a relationship with Uncle Rick!

Bonnie was six before she would go near him.

Fear of the unknown is normal, and shaming a child can block this normal response. So when you introduce your child to any new situation—whether to a stranger or a large family gathering, to solid foods or a potty chair—do it gradually to minimize his anxiety. Forcing him to experience something new will intensify, not alleviate, his fear.

A case in point...

At a Christmas Eve gathering, my one-year-old granddaughter was like a little ship afloat in a sea of adults. Allowed to move freely among us, Jessie looked a little overwhelmed as she went from one adult to the next, but she felt safe because no one demanded hugs and kisses or placed other demands on her. Finally she squeezed in between her parents, the harbor where she was obviously most secure.

Help Structure Your Child's Emotional Experiences

Instead of forcing your child to experience potentially frightening situations or to respond emotionally in a certain manner, help him structure his emotional experiences. The younger your child, the more help he will need. As he grows, he can begin to participate in the process, but while he's an infant, it's up to you.

A case in point...

Whenever I turned on the vacuum cleaner, my three-month-old daughter would wail. I knew the noise scared her, but vacuuming was a normal part of life, and somehow Tabitha had to get used to it.

One day when my mom was visiting, I asked her to take Tabitha to a room at the far end of the house, close the door, and rock and sing to her while I vacuumed. When the muffled noise no longer bothered Tabitha, Mom opened the door and left it ajar. As I worked my way from room to room, I gradually got closer, and by the time I reached the end of the hall, Tabitha was used to the noise. After that she could be in the room where I was vacuuming and not become upset.

Power Points

✓ Stay emotionally grounded.

✓ Be aware of your child's feelings.

✓ Respect his feelings.

✓ Help structure his emotional experiences.

As your child develops language, fantasy and imagination will open up powerful new ways for him to explore his feelings and ideas. At the time of a loss, engaging in activities such as reading, storytelling, artwork, writing, and symbolic play may be less threatening to a child than talking with an adult about what he is feeling. Because children are such great copiers, imaginative play helps them cope with and make sense of painful experiences.

A case in point…

"We'll put an ice pack on it for a couple of minutes," I told my four-year-old daughter, Sara, after she got her first sliver. "That way it won't hurt so much when we take it out."

It was a deep sliver, though, and getting it out of her finger still hurt her. After I finally got it out, I gave her a hug, and she dried her tears and went into her room to play. A little later, I heard her talking to her Mickey Mouse doll, telling him it would hurt but he would feel better after she got his "siver" out.

She played this out for nearly ten minutes before she went on to something else.

In the words of child psychiatrist Bruno Bettleheim, "Play is the royal road to the child's conscious and unconscious inner world; if we want to understand his inner world and help him with it, we must learn to walk this road."[7] This road, however, is not always an easy or obvious one.

> *It should be noted that children at play are not playing about; their games should be seen as their most serious-minded activity.*
>
> MONTAIGNE

When Bobby was three, he fell out of his tree house. He wasn't seriously hurt, but he was badly frightened, and it took some time to help him calm down. A few days later he was playing with one of his action dolls by putting it up on a shelf and pushing it off so that it crashed to the floor. Then he hugged it, put it back on the shelf, and pushed it off again. When his mother heard the doll hitting the floor, she scolded him for not taking care of his toys—and so missed an opportunity to coach him through an emotionally challenging situation.

Fortunately, such situations occur on a daily basis during childhood, and the more you practice feeling talk, the more you'll recognize them as opportunities for emotion coaching. Helping your child learn to self-soothe makes him resilient. It helps him grieve the inevitable losses in life, regulate his behavior in difficult situations, and find the gifts hidden within his losses. The better he becomes at soothing himself, the more strength he'll have to pick himself up after a loss and move confidently into the future.

They do me wrong who say I come no more
when once I knock and fail to find you in;
for every day I stand outside your door,
and bid you wake, and rise to fight and win.

Walter Malone

4

Parting Isn't Such Sweet Sorrow

There's something in the parting hour
Will chill the warmest heart,
Yet kindred, comrades, lovers, friends,
Are fated all to part.

Edward Pollock

Of all the developmental losses of childhood, separation is the first and most traumatic. It begins at birth, when to gain the possibility of life in the world, a newborn must lose the warmth, safety, and security of the womb. As with other life transitions and losses, while the experience of separation leads to grieving, it also provides opportunities for emotional growth.

The Trauma of Birth

Separation at birth is one of the major transitions of life. Preparation for it begins about one month before delivery, when the muscles of the mother's uterus begin to contract and gently massage her unborn infant. This seems to soothe him, and it may even bring him joy. As the baby begins to pass through the birth canal, more intense contractions continue to massage his head and chest, and they travel the entire length of his body, helping to stimulate and initiate many of his physical processes. The hard work of leaving the comfort of his nine-month home leads to distinctive physiological changes that indicate the baby is experiencing stress.

In *Childbirth without Violence*, Frederick Leboyer says that for the infant, birth is at once an escape and a shock. As he struggles through the birth canal, he experiences a tidal wave of sensation, which becomes more and more intense until he is propelled into the light. Leboyer suggests that newborns experience fear and anger in reaction to this trauma and that to minimize the stress on your newborn, you should create as much semblance of continuity with the womb as possible.[8]

We now know that a baby can hear well at birth and that loud noises can scare him. Although a newborn's vision isn't as developed as his hearing, he will squint or close his eyes to avoid bright lights. To increase his sense of safety, unveil his new world as slowly as possible in a sequence of limited revelations. Gently introduce him to one sensation at a time. Soft talk, tender touching, oral stimulation, familiar smells, eye contact, and happy smiles have a positive influence on a newborn. Keeping the lighting dim, the temperature warm, and the room as quiet as possible will minimize the shock and fear he experiences.

Separation Anxiety

Separation begins at birth, but it continues to be a major task throughout life. One of the most common experiences of loss for an infant is separation from his parents. Although some parents choose not to leave their baby at all during the first year, even very brief separations (such as when you take a shower) can trigger fear, anger, and grief. At the heart of raising an emotionally resilient child is helping him learn to calm down when he has been physically aroused by these intense emotions.

For an adult, a period of a few minutes isn't a long time, but it can seem an eternity to a baby. An infant is usually quite vocal when it comes to separations. He may let out a howl, and if he can crawl, he may come searching for you. Think of his behavior as his way of saying that you are his source of security, the most important person in his life right now.

Because his feelings of security are now related less to his environment and more to his internal experience—his memory of you as his secure attachment—your baby really does feel less safe and comfortable when you're not around. And as he becomes more attached to you, he will be less willing to be in the presence of others without you. Both separation anxiety and stranger anxiety are essential to normal development.

Stranger anxiety develops gradually as the baby becomes increasingly aware of what to expect from his surroundings. An infant who doesn't demonstrate a preference for certain people or protest being left alone with a stranger by the end of the first year may have an attachment problem. This can happen with children whose caregivers change many times early in their lives.

If you think there may be attachment problems in your relationship with your baby, you might want to seek help from an early childhood professional who knows how to help parents and young children develop secure relationships. With help, human beings have an amazing capacity to develop an internal sense of security, even if past experiences have not provided that for them. Here are some signs that you and your child may have an attachment problem:

- Your child is older than eighteen months and is as comfortable going to strangers as he is going to you.
- Your child has a hard time giving and receiving affection.
- Your child does not allow you to comfort him when he is hurt or distressed.
- Your relationship with your child is not positive or rewarding.

This doesn't mean that your child has a problem if he doesn't protest when you leave him with a babysitter or grandparent he has come to know and trust. If he's tired, teething, or not feeling well, however, he's likely to object even when you leave him with someone he knows well. Once you're gone, though, he'll be able to use his relationship with the other trusted caregiver to help him through this emotionally challenging experience.

You may find yourself experiencing a range of emotional reactions if your infant cries when he is separated from you. As a loving parent, you may feel guilty that leaving him causes him such distress. You may worry that you have spoiled him, just as Aunt Sally said you would if you picked him up every time he cried. You may fear that you will emotionally damage him if you leave him. To complicate things further, your own childhood experiences with separation or even abandonment may make it hard for you to hear your child's expressions of pain. Finally, you may feel your own sense of loss at having to be separated from your infant, especially if you are leaving him because you have to go to work.

All of these emotions are normal, and recognizing them will help you avoid the negative extremes of denying that your infant's feelings are valid or becoming angry with him for having them. If you fear the feelings that separation engenders in either yourself or your child, you're liable to shut yourself off from them. If you pull away or view your child's feelings as manipulative or attention seeking, it will be nearly impossible for you to support him. Dealing effectively with his separation anxiety requires you to take care of yourself first. If you are angry, depressed, anxious, or fearful when you interact with him, he will feel your emotions, and they can confuse him and add to his distress.

You can validate your infant's experience by not getting caught up in it. Using words and body language, let him know that you understand how he's feeling. Show him that you accept his feelings and that, even though this is hard for him, he will be okay with the help of the person who will care for him in your place. The less anxious and guilty you feel about leaving your baby, the easier it is for him to adjust.

Even though it's emotionally demanding for your baby, separation does not have to damage him. You just need to make sure that you leave him with someone who will create a safe emotional space for him and respond sensitively to his feelings and cues. Over time, as his relationships with alternate caregivers develop, it should become easier for him to be separated from you. He might still prefer your presence and continue to protest at the time of separation, but he will most likely calm down quickly after you leave. If he continues to be upset after you leave or is overly upset with you when you return, you may not have found the best caregiving situation for him.

Helping Your Baby Cope with Separation

Since your infant isn't able to engage in a problem-solving conversation with you, here's how you can structure his experiences to help him cope with separation.

Practice separation through play.

The games you play with your infant can help him understand separation. When he's sitting in his high chair tossing his toys on the floor and fussing until you return them, he's practicing losing and gaining. He will be just as elated after the tenth or twentieth time—if you are that patient—to see the toy reappear. Games such as peekaboo, hide-and-seek, and others that you make up can teach him that people and things still exist even when they are out of sight.

> *A case in point...*
>
> My granddaughter Haley was rocking on her rocking horse in a room adjacent to where I was working on my computer. Every few minutes, the squeaking of the rocker would stop, and Haley would call out, "Amma!"
>
> "Hey, hey, Haley, Haley," I would call back.
>
> Haley would laugh and gleefully return to her rocking.

Use special objects to smooth the transition.

When your infant faces a separation, you can support him by being sure he has his special blanket, teddy bear, or pacifier to help him soothe himself. For him, these objects are linked with thoughts and feelings about you and your home. His "blankie" is his security blanket because it genuinely gives him a feeling of security.

> ### *A case in point…*
>
> One Friday afternoon when Conchita was almost one year old, my husband and I took her to her Nana's for the weekend while we took a short vacation. We brought along her special blanket and one of her cuddly Care Bears. Early Saturday morning we called from the coast, and we called her again on Sunday morning before we headed home.
>
> When we arrived, Nana told us that Conchita had handled the separation like a big girl. Having her favorite things with her and hearing our voices had reassured her that her mama and papa hadn't abandoned her.

Record yourself.

You should talk to your baby long before he can understand words. Talking, singing, or reading to him gives him the comfort he finds in your voice, promotes language development, and teaches him emotional communication skills. Recording yourself reading your baby's favorite stories, singing his favorite songs, or saying reassuring things will keep his memory of you fresh during times of separation.

A case in point...

When Tommy was eleven months old, I was in the navy, and I received orders to go to sea for three months. Jan and I worried that Tommy would forget me and consider me a stranger when I got back.

So before I left, I made a videotape of myself reading him a story and singing a song he liked. Jan put my picture next to Tommy's crib and played the tape every day until I returned. When I got back, Tommy and I were able to reconnect easily.

Help your baby develop relationships with other caregivers. You can prepare your baby for being left with another caregiver by exposing him to other people early in his life, by letting him play with relatives and friends in the safety of your presence, or by leaving him with people you trust for short periods of time.

If you have to go back to work after the birth of your baby, leaving him in the care of one of his grandmothers or another close relative may be the best possible situation for you and him. If this isn't a possibility, you can help him develop a relationship with a new caregiver by using the safety he feels with you as a bridge to trusting another person.

A case in point...

When my son, Ryan, was ten months old, I decided to return to work part time. Once I was sure I had found the right caregiver for him, I deliberately set aside times for

> them to get to know each other when I could be present.
>
> The first time we all got together, I held Ryan in my arms while I talked and laughed with Georgia. I walked around her house with Ryan in my arms, smiling at him and talking to him about this new environment. I showed Georgia one of the games I played with Ryan and watched while she played it with him. While they played, I told her about the other games he liked.
>
> The next time we got together, I left the room for short periods of time, and after a few more visits, I started leaving the house, gradually extending the time I was away until I worked up to the amount of time I would be gone on a regular basis. Every time I left, I would give Ryan a kiss, say "bye-bye," and tell him where I was going and when I would be back.
>
> At first he cried for a while, but by then he was comfortable at Georgia's, and soon his attention focused on other things.

If you gradually prepare your child step-by-step, most likely the transition will go smoothly. But in the event a problem does arise, always leave a phone number where you can be reached. And when you return, give your baby a hug and tell him you're home.

Reconnect after separations.

Reconnecting with your child after separations is important, but it's also challenging. Working parents often feel tired and stressed, and frequently they are so busy with the daily demands of their lives that they don't build in time to reconnect with their children.

An intimate reunion at the end of the day—before the rush to make supper and attend to endless household chores—helps maintain closeness, and children who experience this have fewer problems with their behavior. The best time to establish this practice is when they are infants; if they're older, the sooner you start the better.

A case in point...

When Kasey was a few months old, I began leaving her with a loving caregiver I was lucky enough to find close to where I worked. Since I worked part time, I had to be gone just a few hours at a time, but that was a long time for Kasey.

When I picked her up the first day, I realized that it was important to allow myself time to reconnect with her at the caregiver's. So every day when I arrived to pick her up, I sat on the couch and nursed her while the caregiver told me all about her day. This became an important grounding ritual for us.

It's natural for adults to think about separations from our own perspective of time. If you're separated from your spouse for a week or more because of a business trip, when he returns, you'll doubtless feel the need for special closeness. For your infant, a few hours away from you is a *long* time. When you pick him up from his caregiver's or arrive home after work, allow yourself and him some time to reconnect emotionally. Grabbing the baby bag, strapping him in his car seat, and getting home to make dinner may be your priority, but it's not his. *You* are your baby's priority.

The Importance of Being Honest

Even when your child is an infant, communicate honestly with him. "Good-byes" and "hellos" are as important to him as they are to the adults in your life. Sneaking away raises anxiety in your child, who trusts you as his primary security. By telling him when and where you are going before you put him to sleep, you help him overcome the fear of waking without you. Waiting to leave until he falls asleep may well teach him to fear that you will leave whenever he goes to sleep. Even if he's too young to understand the words, telling him where you are going and when you will return builds trust.

A case in point...

> When José was just a few months old, even if I just had to go outside to hang up the laundry, I would say, "José, I'm going to hang the clothes on the line. I'll be back in a little while. Abuela's here." Then I'd give him a hug, say "bye-bye," and go outdoors. When I returned, I'd give him another hug and say, "Mommy's back, Mijo."

As your child grows older and more verbal, try to return when you said you would, and if you're going to be late, call and tell him when you'll return. Your honesty is the best way to teach your child that he can trust you day by day throughout his life, even in times of loss and grief. Without the trust that honest communication builds, your child may not allow you to help him when he's older.

Power Points

- ✓ Practice separation through play.
- ✓ Use special objects to smooth transitions.
- ✓ Record yourself.
- ✓ Help your baby develop relationships with other caregivers.
- ✓ Reconnect after separations.
- ✓ Tell your child where you are going and when you'll be back.

Every parting gives a foretaste of death, every reunion a hint of the resurrection.

Arthur Schopenhauer

5

Into the Wider World

Strange the world about me lies,
Never yet familiar grown—
Still disturbs me with surprise,
Haunts me like a face half-known.

Sir William Watson

From birth onward, children mature, grow more independent, and move farther away from their parents into a wider and wider world. It is a process of separation that requires the understanding of parents every step of the way.

Toddlers at Work

Everyone has heard about the "terrible twos." Clearly, that description comes from an adult point of view! If two-year-olds were articulate, they'd probably describe themselves as overworked. Having learned to walk, they are prepared to move out into the world. Happily, with this developmental shift comes tremendous energy for exploration and learning about their environment. Between twelve and thirty-six months, toddlers master some of the toughest tasks of their lives.

Separations from you become more complicated, not less. Your toddler still needs you in order to feel secure about his world. In some ways he needs you more than ever. He wants to have the say about when he stays and sits on your lap or when he gets down and explores, but at the same time, the more he explores, the bigger—and more challenging—his world gets. And now *you* want to leave *him?* If you do, he is likely to protest vehemently.

Fortunately, your toddler is also developing abilities that can help him cope with the frustrating emotions separations cause in him. Because of his superb imitative skills at this age, it's important that you don't allow your own distress at times of separation to trigger his fright and tears. He's looking to you for cues about what he should feel. If you communicate your fears about his vulnerability, he could refuse to accept the separations necessary to attend day care or preschool. If you fail to give him credit for what he has gained in being big enough to handle these separations, you can unwittingly allow him the opportunity to behave in manipulative and helpless ways.

All of the strategies for helping infants with separation experiences apply to toddlers as well. In particular, your toddler still needs transitional objects. (As a way of gauging how important these objects are for him, think about how many adults you know who still keep a teddy bear or favorite toy from their baby years.) He also needs your help in developing a relationship with a substitute caregiver. The importance of finding time to reconnect after a separation only increases as your child gets older. As he develops language, you'll be able to talk about the emotions that separation creates for both of you.

> ### *A case in point…*
>
> When Krystal was two and a half, I rode her on the back of my bike to the day-care center and then went to work. One day while we were riding to the center, she asked me to stay with her at day care.
>
> We talked about how we liked being together. Then we talked about how she liked her day-care center, how I liked my job, and how to do those things we had to be apart for a while.
>
> "So," I said, while we waited for a light to change, "it's a glad thing and a sad thing at the same time."
>
> Just talking seemed to make it easier for Krystal to deal with the separation.

More fully shared language also allows you and your child to develop rituals that can help him manage his emotions instead of becoming distraught over separations. Rituals can reassure him that he can handle necessary separations.

> ### *A case in point…*
>
> When Jennifer was two, she began attending a day-care program part time. Even though I had made a gradual transition to this new place and Jennifer had become very

close to the care providers there, she still had a hard time saying good-bye.

Knowing that the day-care program was good for her and that she was safe there, I established a good-bye ritual. After two hugs, two kisses, and two nose kisses, Jennifer would go to the big window inside and watch me walk to the gate outside. Then we'd throw each other a hug and kiss.

Even when Jennifer reached the ripe old age of nine, she and I would still blow each other kisses and send hugs over the phone.

As your toddler begins to move out into the world, you'll quickly discover that he wants to be in control. He wants to figure out the world for himself, and you need to allow him to do so. If you do it for him, he won't learn what he needs to, because at this age he learns directly from experience. It's natural for him to struggle with you about issues of control. In a way, it's his job.

Work is difficult. That's why it's called work.

DAVID BROWN

No is both his favorite and least favorite word. If he's the one using it, it might mean that he's saying it just because he can, that he's refusing to do something, that a task feels too hard for him, or that he doesn't understand what you're asking of him. He could be practicing talking or separateness, or both. If you say no, however, he is likely to respond in frustration to what he interprets as a restriction on his growing independence. He may even throw a tantrum. As unpleasant as tantrums can be, they are excellent opportunities to teach your child feeling talk.

Tantrums Are Opportunities

Most common between eighteen and thirty-six months, tantrums usually occur when a child is overwhelmed by the emotional demands of the moment. When a child throws himself on the floor, kicking, screaming, and crying, he not only feels out of control—he is out of control. At this stage in his development, he lacks the skill he needs to control the feelings precipitated by the frustrating event. When these feelings explode inside him, he cannot control them and so feels scared—terrified—by his own emotions. The overload sends him into a frenzy.

It's hard to reason with a toddler during a tantrum. He is, in fact, beyond reason. Structure the situation so that he can't harm himself or anyone else. Being held helps some children. Hold him and say, "You're upset, and it's okay. I'm going to hold you and keep you safe until you're calm. I'll always love you." Sometimes, however, holding a child just makes the tantrum worse. In that case, you can either ignore him while he vents his feelings or remove him from the stressful area to a quiet place and say, "This is unacceptable behavior."

If exhaustion caused the tantrum, you might just need to help him regain control and let him know that you're there for him. Recognizing his need for rest and consistency in his schedule will help prevent overloads, but sometimes they will occur anyway. Even being hungry may send your child into a tantrum. The better you have learned to recognize your child's behavioral cues, the more likely you'll be able to intervene to help him calm himself.

A case in point…

When Terri was a toddler, she saw sleep as the enemy, and she tried to keep herself from falling asleep by moving faster, running around the room, talking, and laughing. To others in the room, she looked as if she was having a great time, but inevitably she would become overstimulated and overtired—the perfect recipe for a meltdown. So I established bedtime rituals, and when Terri went into overdrive, I pulled her close to nurse or read a book to her.

If the meltdown occurs despite your efforts to prevent it, the first thing you need to do is to become aware of and accept the emotions your child is experiencing. Be as concerned about your child's feelings and desires as you are about his behavior. Listen with empathy. Try to project yourself into his world. View the situation through his eyes to understand what the experience means to him.

You also need to validate his feelings by letting him know that you understand and accept them. The most important component in your child's emotional development is trust—the confidence that he can safely let you know about his feelings and that you will listen, allow him to express them, and respond sensitively. When he knows that, he feels secure and affirmed.

Once you have acknowledged, accepted, and validated his feelings, you can help him further by naming his emotions.

A case in point...

Even before he could speak, our son knew when he was angry. Gabriel knew because my husband and I told him.

"Ooh, that makes you mad," we would groan with enthusiastic empathy. "That really makes you mad."

Then we would stand back and watch an amazing transformation take place before our eyes as a fussing, screeching little person grew quiet, thoughtful, interested.

As often as not, we parents were responsible for creating his frustration in the first place. As I recall, diaper and clothing changes became particularly irksome interruptions during the baby-to-toddler stage. But if we were the villains of this drama, we were also the ones helping to name and legitimize—and ultimately dissipate—the chaotic onslaught of feelings unleashed by any thwarting of toddler will.[9]

This couple didn't seize this "teachable moment" to try to tell their son what they thought was good for him. They were listening with their hearts and responding sensitively to what they heard. The purpose of naming his emotion was to give him a context in which he could begin to understand grief and loss. Capitalizing on an ordinary event of everyday life, they helped Gabriel recognize and work through a little loss so he could begin to develop the skills he would need to eventually cope with larger ones. Naming Gabriel's emotion for him empowered him.

Guiding an infant through an angry outburst may mean walking with him, singing to him, or rocking him until he is calm. Parents often simply know how to do this with babies. But when your infant gets older, you may be more apt to try to distract him. This is not to say there isn't a time and place for using distraction to help your child change his behavior, but when he's having a genuine feeling about something is usually not the time.

If the tantrum is the result of fear, talking calmly may help, but yelling and threatening generally cause a child to feel even more out of control. Even if speaking angrily ends the tantrum, your child will have stopped because of external threats, not because of internal calming.

> *Where the routine is rigorously proscribed by law, the law, and not the man, must have the credit of the conduct.*
>
> WILLIAM H. PRESCOTT

To learn to self-soothe, your child must experience the physiological calming of his emotions within the structure of safety and support you provide. Child psychologist Daniel Hughes describes this process as an "attachment sequence."[10] Linked to the attachment cycle we introduced in chapter 2, an attachment sequence is an interruption of a child's experience of a secure and happy attachment when he does something that elicits your disapproval. In a healthy parent-child relationship, this happens countless times during a child's second year of life. Each sequence ends with a reunion when you assure him that his behavior hasn't damaged your relationship.

Through this sequence, the child increases his sense of independence and autonomy while discovering boundaries, all within the context of a tested, secure relationship. What is critical in a sequence is that you respond with empathy, assign matter-of-fact consequences to his behavior, and then reaffirm your positive and affirming relationship with him.

After the frenzy is over, in other words, you'll need to tell him and show him that you love him. Some parents find that storytelling or reading a book with their child can facilitate reconnecting. You may want to use this reconnecting as an opportunity to talk about feelings and different ways to handle them.

When a tantrum is the result of a your child's anger at you because you set limits on his behavior, you may need to pursue the issue a little later when the incident is in the past and you can talk calmly about his angry feelings and how he might show them in different ways. You might say something like, "I'm really sorry about your behavior. I'm glad you've calmed down so we can talk about how you're feeling now and what you were feeling before." Remember, it's your job to set limits, and it's normal for your child to get angry with you for doing your job.

If you coach your child well through the toddler stage, he might sail through the transition to preschooler. You, on the other hand, might have to deal with your own sense of loss!

A case in point...

My daughter will be turning three this fall, and I can hardly believe it! A part of me rejoices at her emerging independence. I have always felt that giving an infant all the closeness he or she desires can only create a secure, independent child. Watching Mira separate so naturally and joyfully validated my deep inner commitment to the kind of parenting my husband and I have chosen. The part

> of me that loves our new relationship, longs for polysyllabic conversation, and delights in her questions and observations revels in the change.
>
> But another part is not so ready to let go. The all-nurturing, comforting, loving mother-presence inside me is not yet ready to be consigned to mothballs and memories. It is hard for me to make the parenting shift from being all-soothing to setting limits; from giving of myself unstintingly to modeling that mothers also have needs to be considered and honored. And hardest of all is to surrender graciously my place at the center of her life, to step aside as she brushes past me on her way into the world.[11]

Stepping Out

Even as your preschooler steps out, he is still likely to need help coping with separations. As an increasingly verbal and mobile albeit small human being, his initiative and imagination are increasingly important to him. His thinking is greatly influenced by fantasy, and play is guided by how he would like things to turn out. While a preschooler now assimilates information and changes it to fit his existing ideas, later he will learn to change his own ideas to fit new information.

Your child's growing imagination expands his ability to think about what might happen instead of only what is happening. Because of his ability to anticipate order in his world, sudden separations can be very difficult for him. On the other hand, his ability to integrate his emotions, desires, and thoughts gives you an opportunity to help him plan for such events.

Most preschoolers are becoming proficient in using language, so conversations are even more useful than with younger children. You can put this to good advantage by reading books together that help him practice the idea of separating and reconnecting. You can also expand the strategies of talking and reading to include planning and role-playing. If you foresee a separation it helps to role-play ahead of time to help him develop a sense of control over the experience.

A case in point...

Kim and I had planned a trip to the Black Hills. As vacation time approached, we talked with our three-year-old daughter, Carrie, about it and practiced for her stay with her grandmother. Kim got out her suitcase, and Carrie got hers. They chose the clothes they wanted to take and laid them on the bed. Carrie watched carefully to see what her mother packed and then began putting things in her own suitcase. When Kim wrapped her special things in tissue paper, Carrie wrapped her special things in tissue paper, too.

When it came time to leave, Kim, Carrie, and I all carried our own suitcases to the car and climbed inside. As we drove, we talked about how much fun Carrie would have with her grandmother. We talked about how much we would miss each other and how we were already looking forward to getting home to all the hugs and kisses we would share.

At my mom's house, we all got out of the car and went inside. After a few minutes, while Carrie played with Mom's cat, Fluffy, Kim and I said good-bye to Mom. Then we called Carrie and hugged and kissed her good-bye. Later, Mom told us that as soon as we drove off, Carrie went looking for Fluffy again.

Starting preschool is a big step, one that can affect a child's attitude toward school for years to come. By the time most children reach the preschool years, they have experienced separations from primary caregivers, and many will have been in day-care programs long before reaching preschool age. Because of their continued interest in the world and their desire for new experiences, many of them look forward to preschool.

However, some preschoolers are more cautious and might not want to be separated from their parents. To cope with separation experiences, they may need the same kind of support as toddlers. Your child may regress in some ways for a while. When he gets home the first few times, he may be angry, cranky, or just plain tired.

In general, separations are easier for this age group than for infants and toddlers, and that makes your experience as primary caregiver or parent less stressful. Just be sure you plan ahead and prepare your child for the change.

A case in point...

Jan and I planned very carefully for Danny's transition to preschool. We gathered information about how to pick a preschool and prepare for this change. With the help of our support system, we made a list of likely schools, and then we visited and evaluated each one. The one we chose had a calm, relaxed atmosphere, a good ratio of caregivers to students, an abundance of creative opportunities, a clean facility, and a warm, knowledgeable staff.

> Danny and I visited the local library. He chose some books about going to preschool, and over the next few weeks we read them during our quiet times together. Danny repeatedly insisted that we drive by "his school." We talked and role-played with him.
>
> After he started preschool, Danny felt taxed at first, but we helped him dress in the mornings if he needed us to, and we kept his schedule as steady as possible and made sure he got plenty of rest.
>
> It wasn't long before Danny could hardly wait for the big yellow school bus to arrive in the morning.

From leaving the womb to entering preschool, separation is a major transition for your child, and he will need your help. At each stage, you'll need to be sensitive to what he is experiencing, be available to comfort and help soothe him, give him the space to grieve, and be honest with him. If you do your part, he will adjust to this transition and enjoy what he gains from his losses—increased independence, self-confidence, and new social skills.

Power Points

- ✓ Talk about the emotions that separation creates for both of you.
- ✓ Name you child's emotions.
- ✓ Use tantrums as opportunities to practice feeling talk.
- ✓ Develop reassuring rituals.

There are gains for all our losses,
there are balms for all our pains.

Richard Henry Stoddard

6

A Season of Loss

And after summer evermore succeeds barren winter,
with his wrathful nipping cold:
so cares and joys abound, as seasons fleet.

SHAKESPEARE

In addition to separation, children face other losses as they pass through the seasons that turn them from infants into preschoolers. The developmental milestones of weaning and toilet training lead to significant gains as children attain more control over their bodies and greater access to the people and things in the world.

In different cultures, and in different families within a culture, these events occur in different ways and at different ages for a child. The focus here, however, is not on the details of these normal developmental events, but on a child's emotional response to them. Even normal transitions require children to adjust to a new way of life, and adjustment requires grieving for what is lost. A child who is allowed to experience his feelings about normal losses will grow in emotional strength and resilience and develop the basic skills of good grieving—the natural healing process of resolving all loss.

Weaning

Whether you are weaning from the breast or the bottle, your child is losing something that has been a source of nurturance and comfort for him. Although sucking is the way infants receive nutrition, it's also one of the primary ways they self-soothe. That's why losing the opportunity to suck is like a double whammy. Not only is it a big loss in itself, but it also involves a behavior your child has previously used to soothe himself when he experienced uncomfortable feelings.

So when you wean your child, it's very important to come up with other self-soothing routines. As he experiences the soothing you provide through rocking, massage, or other shared rituals, he will learn new ways to self-soothe. That, in turn, will make him much better at controlling his behavior in response to negative emotions and more resilient in the face of loss in the future.

As is true for all developmental milestones, there is no absolute time to wean. The differences among mother-child relationships make set time lines useless. Across cultures, a vast range of durations is considered appropriate.

> *I have stilled and quieted my soul; like a weaned child with its mother, like a weaned child is my soul within me.*
>
> Psalm 131:2

In the United States, for example, the "rules" about how long to nurse have changed radically within just fifty years—from "let the child nurse until the next baby is born" to "wean from the breast at six months (or earlier)" to "nurse until the preschool stage." American mothers have been pulled in many directions. Perhaps the wisest course is to wean when both the mother and child are ready. T. Barry Brazelton writes:

> The only reason I'd urge weaning would be if it were interfering with [the child's] becoming independent. But if she is autonomous in all other domains, the closeness is all to the good. I've studied cultures where mothers breast feed the new baby on one breast and the other children up to five years of age on the other.... The children do fine, but the mothers look haggard.[12]

The trick is to be in touch with both your child's and your own needs so you recognize when it's time. Just remember that sucking has provided a powerful soothing experience for your baby. This makes stopping especially trying for him, and it will engender feelings of loss. If your child is older, he may even be able to articulate those feelings.

A case in point...

My daughter stopped nursing the day after her third birthday. We had talked about stopping. Even though she wanted to continue, my milk was drying up. Although we had prepared for this day for over a month, she was still very sad when the day came, and for several days she cried over small things. She had a very hard time letting me hold

> her because then she wanted to nurse, so she pushed away from me.
>
> I also felt sad and somewhat alienated from her during this time. It was a hard time for both of us. I felt guilty about not having enough milk to be able to continue to nurse her, and I felt sad at the lost closeness, even though I also felt freer.
>
> Although I knew that she was sad and more irritable than usual, I did not realize the extent of her angry feelings until several months later when, one day, she said to me, "Mommy, remember when I was three and you didn't nurse me anymore and I wanted to break all my toys and you wouldn't let me?"
>
> There had been no outward attempts to hurt her toys, and I'd had no idea of the degree to which she had been angry, but clearly anger was also a part of her experience of grieving.

You, too, must be up to the change. After all, both of you will suffer loss. A nursing mom's experience was captured well in the comic strip "Baby Blues." Mom and Dad are in the bathroom talking about their day as they get ready for bed.

"Oh!" Mom says, "I forgot to tell you—Hammie refused to be breast-fed today!"

"Really?" Dad asks with a grin. Then he gives his wife a big hug.

"I think he's ready to completely switch to solid food," Mom adds.

"That's great!" says Dad. Then he heads off to bed.

In the final frame, Mom is sitting on the floor in front of the sink, sobbing.

Let's face it: Both mom and baby are likely to miss the unique closeness and intimacy nursing creates. On the positive side of this transition, your baby will have taken a step toward independence as he learns to feed himself, and if you were breast-feeding, you will have taken a step toward greater freedom.

For your baby's comfort and your own, use all the emotional coaching skills you learned and practiced with early separations. Recognize and validate his signals of grieving. He may be more irritable and need more physical contact and holding. If you recognize the loss he's experiencing, you can provide the comforting he needs to get through this developmental transition. Choose your timing with care, approach the process gradually, and watch for his signals. Take care of yourself, and call on your support system when you need to.

A case in point...

Part of the bedtime ritual for Sammy and me was lying down together so she could nurse. By the time she was two and a half, she nursed only three times a day, so it seemed a good time to wean her. Dropping the morning nursing happened naturally, and I shifted to playing with her or reading to her as a way of reconnecting after work. However, my attempt to make the transition at bedtime by lying with her and listening to music was futile. No longer allowed to nurse, Sammy became restless and irritated.

To solve the problem, my mother, who lived with us, lay down with Sammy in the evenings and listened to soft music with her before bedtime. It took three months before I could take part in the new nighttime ritual.

If you wait to wean until your child is a preschooler, it will be both harder and easier. What makes it harder is that both you and your child will have become more attached and accustomed to nursing. What makes it easier is that the increasing importance of peer relationships to your preschooler provides a definite pull away from the breast or bottle. Further, the sophisticated use of language typical of children between the ages of three and five makes explaining the process easier than with a baby or toddler. It also makes it easier to comfort him through the loss as he finds new ways to self-soothe.

Power Points

✓ Provide your baby with new opportunities for self-soothing.

✓ Wean him when both you and he are ready.

✓ Approach the process gradually.

Toilet Training

Few early achievements can compete in degree of satisfaction and pride for both parent and child like the completion of toilet training. As with successful separation and weaning, toilet training involves losses and gains. The bowel and bladder control required for successful toilet training means the loss of the unfettered freedom of infancy. Minor as it may seem to adults, having to stop what he is doing and go to a specific place to relieve his bladder or bowel is a major change for a child.

On balance, however, one kind of freedom is lost and another gained for mother and child alike. In the words of child advocate and author Penelope Leach, "Toilet training is not a question of making the child do something for you. It is a matter of helping him do something for himself. You are not training him to potty or toilet but helping him to take independent charge of his own functions."[13]

> *Perhaps the most valuable result of all education is the ability to make yourself do the thing you have to do, when it ought to be done, whether you like it or not.*
>
> THOMAS HUXLEY

Nowadays, there's a strong consensus that it's preferable not to attempt toilet training until a child is two. However, a growing minority of parents have taken the opposite tack, effectively beginning toilet training a few months, or even weeks, after childbirth.

Borrowing from patterns that work remarkably well in other cultures, these parents don't diaper their children at home. Instead, they stay close so they can keep an eye on them. The ongoing parent-child dance of attachment, which involves an ever-growing awareness of each other, can enable you to know when your child might be ready to void. Then you can take him to the toilet and, in an easygoing, playful fashion, encourage him to "do his business."

Which is right? Waiting until after two or starting at six months? Both are right in the sense that both ways can work, but one will work better depending on the parent-child pair. Rules handed down over the ages may or may not work in your situation or with your child's temperament. It's important for you to assess the fit for yourself. Ultimately, you are the expert in what works best because you are there to see the results.

Parents fortunate enough to have sufficient resources to allow one parent to be home with the child full time may elect to begin early. Parents whose busy schedules and myriad responsibilities don't allow for the close and constant contact required for early toilet training may find it wiser to begin the process when the child is beginning to want the independence that being diaper-free brings. Here we consider three strategies that are useful for children from two to five years of age.

1. Be sensitive.

The first thing you need to do is to be sensitive to what else is going on in a child's life.

> *A case in point...*
>
> Just as three-year-old Jimmy was nearly toilet trained, I got a big promotion and transfer to Hawaii. My wife, Jill, and I were thrilled and excited, and Jimmy felt happy, too, until we started packing everything up and nothing was where it was supposed to be. As the confusion and chaos increased, Jimmy's little world turned upside down, and he started to have lots of accidents.
>
> We understood what was happening and talked with him. I said, "Jimmy, you've been doing a great job with the potty, but it's so busy around here right now that we're all

doing too many things. Let's wait until we get to our new house to use the potty, okay? You can wear diapers until then."

As soon as we were settled in our new house and had reestablished our normal daily routines, Jimmy did well with his potty training.

2. Be flexible.

Being flexible is extremely important in all aspects of parenting, and there's no question that moving is one of the situations in life that require us to change our plans. At such times, the most important thing is not to adhere to a rigid plan, but to find the very best way to meet your child's need for emotional security, which doesn't change.

A case in point...

My brother Peter and his wife, Ann, had moved a year before we did. Not wanting to spoil their three-and-half-year-old daughter, they continued with potty training. When Kathrin had accidents, Ann became angry because she thought Kathrin wasn't trying. The strain between her and her mother resulted in Kathrin's throwing tantrums, and six months after the move, she was still having accidents.

When we learned that we, too, would be moving, Jill and I remembered how insisting on sticking to potty training had caused such frustration for everybody in Peter's family, and we decided there had to be a better way.

Both Kathrin's and Jimmy's parents meant well. The difference was that Kathrin's parents didn't realize that she *was* trying and that her accidents were her way of reacting to the loss of her normal routine. Nothing important to her was where she could find it. She wasn't being stubborn; she was trying as hard as she could, but it became extremely hard for her to keep up the effort and concentration needed to potty train. In addition to feeling awful about her move-related losses, she was feeling bad about the accidents. They made her feel like a baby—and she didn't like that one bit!

3. Be open.

One of the best strategies for toilet training is to prepare your child for it by talking comfortably about elimination and sexuality with him from the time he is born. These two essential body functions are closely related, and in due course, your child will need to learn to handle them appropriately. However, many parents find it difficult to speak about these topics, even to other adults.

If that describes you, your discomfort may come from a lack of experience in talking about them, or perhaps from memories of when you were a baby yourself and your parents smiled when you found and named your ears, mouth, and nose, but frowned when you touched and explored your genitalia. Even greater discomfort may have been created if your parents slapped your hands away, punished you, or said things like "Bad boy!" or "No, no!"

Your child needs to accept these functions as normal to be able to accept himself. Even using expressions like "yucky" and "peuw," or making faces that convey disgust or displeasure, can send the message that some body functions are not good. When you are open and comfortable in communicating with your young child about them, you teach him that he can talk with you about anything. This open communication can start early and easily with diaper changes and baths.

A case in point...

Whenever I changed his dirty diaper, I could see that James was watching me, so I made sure that I smiled and that my expression was relaxed and accepting. I always spoke in a kind tone of voice.

I did the same thing at bath time. I washed all parts of his body gently, explaining as I went. "You'll like this warm washcloth on your tummy," I'd tell him. "Next we'll wash your penis."

James's reaction showed me that he felt just as comfortable having a dirty diaper changed as he did having both his tummy and penis washed.

His father's positive comments and reactions made James feel comfortable in his body. He sensed that its functions were okay and that he was okay. This kind of sensitive responding sets the stage for open and honest communication about feelings connected with other normal parts of the life cycle, including death.

Power Points

✓ Take into account everything going on in your baby's life.

✓ Stay flexible.

✓ Talk openly about elimination and sexuality.

Whether you are weaning or toilet training your child, the more you use your guidance skills, consider the timing, remain flexible and sensitive to the challenge the transition poses for him, and communicate honestly and openly with him, the easier these necessary changes will be for the entire family.

Our heavenly Father never takes anything from His children unless He means to give them something better.

George Müeller

7

Hello!

We haven't all had the good fortune to be ladies;
we haven't all been generals, or poets, or statesmen;
but when the toast works down to babies,
we stand on common ground.

Mark Twain

Some childhood losses aren't related to developmental milestones such as separation, weaning, and toilet training. Nevertheless, they are very common, and you need to know how to help your child grieve and get through them. One change that can be particularly taxing for a child is the birth of a sibling.

For children who already have siblings, the arrival of a new baby won't be as great a shock as it will for a child who has previously been the only one. As the middle child in a very large family, I don't recall ever being jealous or angry when a new baby came home to the farm, maybe because, being the seventh child, the six that followed seemed like normal events. For an only child, however, the arrival of an "intruder" can be a traumatic event. It requires a lot of skill and effort on the part of parents for their firstborn to experience this event as a blessing, because from his point of view the change isn't for the better. What to the rest of the family is a gain to him is a loss.

You Ain't Seen Nothin' Yet!

Remember what it was like when your first baby was born?

Well, you ain't seen nothin' yet!

All the stress and strain of the first months of sleeplessness recur with the arrival of a second child, and in addition you have another little one whose need for attention doesn't diminish just because you are depleted from the new demands. Your time will be at a premium, and you will be taxed to the limit. During this time, you'll find that planning pays off.

If your first child is still an infant, his reactions will depend entirely on how much his routine is affected. That's why taking care of yourself first is essential. If you aren't rested and emotionally grounded, you won't be able to meet the increased demands that the pregnancy and birth will place on you. But if you are physically fit, rested, and emotionally upbeat, your infant probably won't even know that something major has just happened.

Once the newborn is home, the closer to the usual routine things stay for the firstborn, the less disruption he will experience and the less distress he will signal. Likewise, the more changes that occur during pregnancy and after the birth, the more losses he will experience in the form of less attention, less soothing, and the disruption of his routine. Calling on all the resources available to you and letting your support system help will keep things on a more even keel. Give those you trust a chance to help, and be willing to ask for what you need—a home-cooked meal for the family, transportation, a sounding board or wise counsel, care for your baby, or help with housework.

Having someone you trust give you respite from parenting your young children for brief periods is an incredible gift, as it gives you the opportunity to take care of some of your physical and emotional needs. This includes time to nurture the relationship with your partner so that you stay connected on the parenting journey.

A World Turned Upside Down

Unlike an infant, even in the best of circumstances a toddler will be very aware that his world has just been turned upside down. It's impossible for things to remain the same when a new baby arrives. The newborn's needs will disrupt the older child's established sleeping, eating, and playing time, and it will be hard for him to count on anything anymore. He will feel a loss of his position as the one and only child in the family, and he will intensely miss the time and quality of attention he is used to.

One of the ways you can help prepare your toddler for the birth of a sibling is simply to talk about it. When the pregnancy starts to show, begin to tell him that a new baby is coming. Repetition helps.

> *A case in point...*
>
> When I began to show, I told my daughter, Judy, that I was going to have a baby. In response to her questions, I explained that the baby was growing in my tummy and that when it was big enough, it would come out and be born, and then she would have a little brother or sister.

I encouraged her to put a hand on my tummy to feel the baby moving and kicking inside. I also let her talk to the baby. During my pregnancy, Judy proudly pointed to my tummy and announced to friends and strangers alike, "Baby in here."

Get out your firstborn's baby book and show him how he has grown. Remind him what fun you and he had, and tell him how cute he was. Talk about having a new baby and read him books about babies. And don't forget to tell him often, "We love you lots."

Toddlers are more verbal and mobile than infants, so they are increasingly able to participate in and understand what is happening.

A case in point...

Amber turned three while I was pregnant with her brother. I made changes gradually so she didn't have to deal with everything at once. I told her it was time for her to have a big-girl bed. We talked about the new bed for weeks before we bought it, and she helped pick out the bedding. When the new bed came, she jumped up and down on it with glee.

On the first night she was to sleep in her new bed, Amber nestled on it with me, and I read her two of her favorite stories as we cuddled. Before she drifted off to sleep, she whispered, "I miss my crib."

"I know," I whispered back.

As my delivery date approached, I took Amber to the

hospital to show her where the baby and I would be, and she went with her dad and me to shop for things for the baby. To help prepare her to be a big sister, Santa brought her a baby doll that needed bottle-feeding, bathing, and diapering.

When the birth is imminent, tell your toddler exactly what to expect, and prepare him for unexpected changes in plans.

A case in point…

Just before her baby brother was born, I told my daughter exactly what to expect:

"Cari, when the new baby is born, Tía Rita will come and be here with you. I'll take Mommi to the hospital and stay there with her. After the baby is born, you and Tía Rita can come and see Mommi, Poppi, and the baby, and then you will come home again. Poppi will stay with Mommi overnight in the hospital, and you will stay with Tía Rita. You can call Mommi, and she will call you. I will call you, too, and we can all talk. Mommi and I and the baby will all come home after you get up the next morning."

Just in case there was extended labor or a complication with delivery, I planned ahead to call Cari on the phone. We also planned to spend some cuddly time with her to let her know how special she was to us before Tía Rita arrived and we left for the hospital.

Giving your toddler a special gift upon the occasion of the new baby's homecoming can help, as can having someone else carry the newcomer so that you can focus on your toddler. Judith's daughter, now a mother herself, still remembers when her newborn brother arrived home from the hospital. From her point of view at two and a half, her mother was so eager to hug her that she *threw* the baby at her dad.

The first few days your newborn is home are very important ones for your toddler. He needs special time with you to be reassured of your love. Take him to a park while the baby, who is "too little to play," stays home with grandmother or another trusted caregiver.

> ### *A case in point...*
>
> I had given my sixteen-month-old son, Ben, a set of play tools for Hanukkah. He loved to hammer the pegs into the holes just like I hammered nails when I worked in the garage.
>
> One day when Ben's new baby brother was just home from the hospital and especially fussy, Ben began whining. So I swooped him up in my arms, grabbed his play tool set, and took him to the garage, where the two of us spent the rest of the afternoon "building things"—things the new baby was too little to know about.

Once the baby is home, talk to your toddler about his feelings of being sad and left out, and cuddle and rock him or engage in some other special activity that emphasizes how much you still love him. Your acceptance of his neediness will help him tolerate not only his new sibling, but also higher levels of stress in his life.

It isn't at all unusual for a child this age to throw temper tantrums or show other signs of emotional distress. He might even regress and start to suck his thumb again, have more accidents with potty training, and cling and cry more than usual. He may want to nurse or have his bottle back. This is normal, so don't be concerned. Find ways to distract him from nursing, but otherwise tolerate his backpedaling. His need to be held and cuddled more indicates that he is distressed and in need of soothing.

The adjustment is most difficult for everyone when a baby is born into a family with a one- to three-year-old toddler who hasn't yet reached the point where it's possible for him to share. At this stage of development, the operative word is *mine*. So imagine your toddler's utter frustration at having to share your attention, time, and love with someone else. Having to share previously exclusive love and attention will feel like a profound loss and may result in outbursts of intense anger and jealousy.

For you, the difficulty lies in having an infant while your other child is going through the terrible twos, which as we have already seen, is a monumental undertaking in itself. The best way to make the situation better for everyone is to draw on your support system. Once home from the hospital, call on everyone you know and trust to help out. They will usually be happy to assist, and their help will make all the difference in your family's ability to manage this transition successfully.

Aggressive gestures toward the newborn, which are not at all unusual, provide excellent opportunities for you to use feeling talk to help your child grieve his losses while still setting firm limits.

A case in point...

When Cameron pinched his newborn sister, I took him aside and said, "I know the new baby takes a lot of our time and that you must feel left out, but hurting your baby sister is a no-no. We love you and we will take care of you. It's okay for you to feel mad, but it's not okay to hurt your baby sister because you feel mad."

Listen to your child's anger, but do not accept meanness. Tell him when his behavior hurts other people. Tell him that what he did or said was mean and that it makes you sad. If his behavior is not self-correcting, it has to cost him something.

> *Logical consequences are the scarecrows of fools and the beacons of wise men.*
>
> THOMAS HUXLEY

If your toddler feels insecure about his place in the family or because of his parents' love for the new baby, sibling rivalry may become an issue. It will be very difficult initially for your toddler to have positive feelings for the new baby, much less love him. But in time, as he becomes convinced that he is still important to you, he will gradually warm up to his new sibling. Including him as much as possible in activities with the new baby will increase their bonding and help him continue to feel like an essential part of your expanded family.

Ready for Responsibility

Helping your preschooler cope with the birth of a sibling means taking advantage of the developmental skills he has acquired. His motor skills are much more developed, and he is able to participate in more family activities. His verbal skills have greatly increased as well, so communication is easier for both of you. Because of his intense focus on mastery and being "older," giving him tasks that let him show his competence provides him with excellent techniques for coping. With careful preparation and a good sense of himself and his place in the family, a preschooler can begin bonding with a newborn sibling sooner than most toddlers can.

A case in point...

I took care of my grandson Joey when his little brother was born. Joey visited his mom and the new baby in the hospital, and when he got back, he told me all about his experience.

"First I got to go upstairs to Mommy's room, and she let me get on the bed with her. The little baby was in his crib by Mommy's bed. Then Mommy said I could hold him, and so I did. Mommy picked him up and gave him to me, and I got to hold him for a long, long time. And he didn't cry or nothin'. He's my little brother."

Plan a shopping trip for the new baby's needs, and allow your preschooler to pick out a little gift for the baby and one for himself. Let him help with chores at home to give him a feeling of responsibility. When the birthing time approaches, include him in the planning. He is able to understand a hospital visit before the real thing happens, and if there's a choice about who will care for him, let him have a vote.

Once the new baby comes home, your preschooler can help with any number of little tasks that need doing. Using this season of loss as an opportunity to teach him responsibility is one of the best gifts you can give him. Giving him important tasks will help you and will allow him to grow into his new role as big bother and responsible older child. Bathing, diapering, dressing, and feeding the baby under your supervision will make him feel needed and special in his new role in the family.

When you assign your preschooler chores and ask for his help, however, be sure he doesn't take on more than he can handle. There's a delicate balance between feeling needed and feeling overwhelmed with responsibility, and a preschooler is the last one to recognize his limits. That's your job. Not only must you identify the tasks he can and cannot do, but you also need to explain to him the dangers of trying to do too much. Much as he might want to show his new baby sister his love by picking her up and carrying her around, you need to make sure it doesn't happen when you're not there to supervise.

After all the chores of the day are done and baby is settled in the crib, take a little time for some "big boy" fun, like building a puzzle or reading a story or chatting by the fire. "You really did a lot to help Mommy today. You got the diapers and the wipes and helped me fold the clothes. You even answered the phone when I was busy with the baby. It sure was nice to have such a big boy around today. I bet you're feeling real grown-up tonight!"

Even with the best preparation, though, there may be times when your preschooler feels distressed, angry, or jealous. He's been in the family long enough to know the roles, and after being "king of the hill" for four years or so, it seems to him that an upstart is challenging his turf. The new baby cries and disturbs him and the rest of the family while you're watching TV, eating dinner, or trying to sleep at night. Your preschooler might well say something like, "I'm tired of this baby. I think it's time to send her back."

Love is as strong as death,
its jealousy unyielding as the grave.
SONG OF SONGS 8:6

To help your preschooler get over feelings of jealousy, you might show him how many more things he can do now than he could when he was a baby. You might cut out pictures and make collages together, one of what a baby can do and another of what he can do. A baby can only crawl and sit up, but he can walk and jump and run and swing on swings. You could also make a third collage of the things that both a baby and he can do, such as smile and laugh, feel sad and cry.

Fatigue, tension, hunger, and excitement can max out your preschooler, and he may burst into tears over little events. Nightmares can be another sign of overload. Three- to five-year-olds do not yet have the emotional strength and flexibility to handle strong feelings, and loss can overwhelm them.

When your preschooler is flooded with feelings and the excitement has grown too much for him, he will need your sensitivity, empathy, and emotion coaching. Acknowledging, accepting, and naming his feelings will make a real difference. Taking the time to hold him and tell him you love him, especially when he is tired or growing overwhelmed, will help him manage the transition and develop emotional resilience.

It's a good idea to have a few gifts stashed away to give your preschooler when others make a fuss over the adorable new baby. Keep an eye out for ways you can show your child how special he is. Let him sit in your lap or stay near you. Keep your arm around him. He may feel that he won't get his share of love, so reassure him that you have plenty of it to go around.

A case in point...

When I was four and a half, my cousin Jo Ellen and I went to the mountains to visit Grandma. We had a good time playing together and being with our special grandmother.

One day, Jo Ellen said, "I love you, Gran."

"How can you love Grandma when I love her?" I asked.

Grandma put one arm around each of us and hugged us to her. "See, I love you both, and you both love me. Isn't it wonderful that God made us so we can have enough love for everyone?"

Regardless of the age of your child when a new baby joins the family, you need to maintain a routine that keeps his life as predictable as possible and make special time to remind him that he's still loved. It's also important to accept, acknowledge, and name feelings of anger, jealousy, and abandonment. Place firm limits on aggressive behavior toward the newborn while giving the older child lots of snuggling and cuddling to help him get through the loss.

Power Points

- ✓ Tell your child that a new baby is on the way.
- ✓ Read books to him about babies.
- ✓ Tell him what to expect.
- ✓ Let him help.
- ✓ Reassure him that you love him.
- ✓ Tolerate regressive behavior.

What's the use of a newborn child?
To raise the dead heart? To set wild the fettered hope?

Witter Bynner

8

Good-Bye!

I'm sure no human heart goes wrong
That's told "Good-bye—God bless you!"

Eugene Field

Moving and the death of a pet are other common losses children experience from birth through age five. Moving is emotionally exhausting, and most often everyone in the family will grieve the loss of the old home, although in different ways. The death of a pet is an even harder loss for a child, especially if it's his first experience with death—a permanent and irretrievable loss.

Moving

The distance moved, the attachment to the old house and neighborhood, and the degree of similarity between the old and the new all influence how family members experience and grieve the losses a move entails. The most important factor for children, however, is their stage of development, for that will determine what the loss means to them and what skills they can call on to help them cope.

Infants

The easiest time for children to move is when they are infants. That's because their primary attachments are to the people who will move with them, and making friends isn't yet a developmental task. You are your infant's exclusive concern, and his emotional response to the move, if any, depends on how you handle your own feelings. He reacts to the world through you, and his responses are based entirely on your emotional state. If your stress rubs off on him, it can upset him.

The most important thing is for his routine to stay as it was before the move. Limiting changes to the move itself will make things easier for him. Keep his things as undisturbed as possible during the move, and once you're in the new house, set up his room first.

Planning your move can minimize the distress associated with this transition. The more distant the move, the more you need to plan. If the move is disorganized, you're apt to become tired and anxious. Take care of yourself, and lean on your support system to help you in whatever ways they can at both ends of the move. Grandparents can be a great help, either by caring for your baby when you feel overwhelmed, or by freeing you up to do other things essential for the move.

Don't be surprised if you note regressive behaviors such as increased fussiness. They are simply indications that your child is reacting to the move. If they occur, accept his need to be held, and spend extra time with him—as challenging as that may be. Reassure him physically, with lots of snuggling and cuddling, and verbally, with repeated words and sounds of comfort and consolation.

Toddlers

In addition to the stress always associated with moving, you have a little bundle of needs tagging after you with demands for affection and attention. This can be exhausting. If you have begun weaning or toilet training, don't feel obligated to continue with it. It will likely just create more stress for both of you.

Toddlers are much more attached to familiar surroundings than infants are, but their attachments to their friends aren't as strong as they will be later. At this developmental stage, playing with friends simply means that they play at the same time. They don't really play together. What you convey to your toddler emotionally and the degree of continuity you provide him are still the most important things you can do to help him make the transition successfully.

You can use more explicit strategies with a toddler than you can with an infant. Reading him a book about moving can give him some of the extra attention he craves as well as provide additional structure for the change. You can also support him by acknowledging, naming, and allowing him to express his feelings.

A case in point...

When Felipe was twenty-eight months old, I was transferred to a new job far enough away that we had to move. Before the move, Rosa and I talked about how everything would have to be packed up and how long the trip would be. We visited our new house. The night before the big move, while I was tucking Felipe into bed, he asked, "Will I cry?"

"You'll feel sad, " I said. "And it's okay to cry."

When he got to the new house, at first Felipe ran around, totally excited about his new surroundings, especially the swimming pool. Then suddenly he threw himself on the floor and began to cry. "I wanna go home!" he sobbed.

I sat down beside him and rubbed his back. "You know," I said, "I feel really sad about leaving, too. I really loved that old house!"

> *That familiar indefinable lump in the chest...leaving houses...any place that you had made with difficulty and affection your home. In fact, simply going away.*
>
> ANNE MORROW LINDBERGH

Preschoolers

Preschoolers have a much stronger attraction to familiar people, places, and things than younger children do. Unlike toddlers, they play interactively, and their playmates are important to them. Losing friends and a neighborhood at the same time can be very difficult for them.

A case in point...

Janie was three when we decided to move across town to a new neighborhood. Before the move, we visited our new house many times and met some of our neighbors. We took pictures of the house and put them on the refrigerator in the old house, and I put a big calendar low on the refrigerator door and let Janie cross off each day so she could tell how close the big day was.

After we were pretty well settled in our new home, we were reminiscing about our friends in the old neighborhood. Janie was strangely quiet.

"You know," I said, "I'm feeling kind of homesick. How about if we jump in the car, drive by our old house, and visit the Johnsons? Janie, you could play with your friend Heidi."

On the way home, my husband said, "Sure was nice to see John and his family, wasn't it, honey?"

"Yes," I replied, "and our old house, too. How about you, Janie?"

"Me too!" she said.

For a preschooler, talking about feelings is an essential part of good grieving. Share your own feelings of loss and sadness about this change, and try as hard as possible not to pass on your stress or anxiety to him. As his feelings shift from sadness to excitement about the new adventure, he will learn that emotions change and that feeling them and talking about them are okay. Instead of trying to rescue him from his feelings, be alert for opportunities to name and validate them.

Talk about the move, too. The more you talk about it, the easier it will be for him to know what to expect and the less frightening it will be. Playing or doing artwork with him will help structure the discussion and provide him with alternate ways to communicate. Talk about meeting new friends, going to a new school, and sharing the exciting things about the new home.

Plan a gradual transition. With each family conference, give your preschooler more information about packing chores, the movers, and the location of and details about the new house. Involve him as much as possible in the preparations and help structure the experience by planning activities that will help him get through the difficult times.

A case in point...

My husband had worked for a company for many years when he was transferred to another state. Shortly after we learned of the transfer, he and I called a family meeting to introduce the plan to five-year-old Amy.

"Daddy has a new job in San Diego," I said. "See on the map, here. That's where it is, right by the ocean. We'll be able to play on the beach and make sand castles in the summertime. Our new house will be bigger than this one, and it will have a big backyard for you to play in with your new friends."

We made several trips to the new house and spent a Saturday at the beach. It was a little cool for me, but Amy thought it was wonderful. We visited the San Diego Zoo and Amy's new school, and I helped her memorize her new address and telephone number.

Before we moved, Amy and I visited all our favorite places in the old neighborhood and took pictures of her friends. She had a good-bye party, and she gave each of her guests a self-addressed postcard she had made. Amy's friends all told her they would write on the postcards and send them to her, and Amy said she would write back.

Even though everyone might be excited and looking forward to the move, prepare your youngster for the hectic adventure it will be. Moving doesn't always go according to plan, so let your preschooler know that there may be surprises or disappointments—the moving van might be late, or the power may not have been turned on at the new house.

Moving tends to bring out the worst in everyone, so warn your preschooler that you might get upset. You might become worried and snap, "Stay out of the driveway and street!" Dad might holler, "Where in the world did you pack my shoes?" Assure him that as soon as things settle down again (and they will settle down again!), everything will be okay. Everyone will recover, although apologies might be called for.

A case in point...

My daughters, five-year-old Ellen and two-year-old Blair, were playing in the hallway of our new home. Their room was all set up just the way they liked it, but they didn't want to play there. Instead, they wanted to be where the action was, so they dragged some things out into the hall and played with them there.

Suddenly I rushed around the corner. I slipped on a small plastic car and almost fell.

"This is a mess!" I yelled. "You two are acting like a couple of two-year-olds!"

Ellen thought for a moment and then said, "Blair is two, Mommy."

I looked at Ellen, then at Blair, and then at Ellen again.

"I'm sorry," I said. "I'm giving myself time-out in my room so I can settle down."

It is very easy to forgive others their mistakes.
It takes more guts and gumption to forgive
them for having witnessed your own.

JESSAMYN WEST

If you move while your child is in this age group, you have your work cut out for you, so remember to call on your old support system and start creating a new one even before you move. Setting up a new support system requires time and energy, but the more you work on it, the easier the move will be for you and your preschooler. Referrals from doctors, dentists, and teachers to professionals in the new area can ease the transition into a new community, but finding the right school and neighborhood in a new town or state can be difficult without some local support.

POWER POINTS

- ✓ Provide as much continuity as possible.
- ✓ Control the stress level.
- ✓ Set up a new support system.

The Death of a Pet

Infants

In itself, the death of a pet will have almost no impact on an infant because he doesn't have the cognitive capacity to grasp the concept of death. Your baby's entire world is about his attachment to you. But as his primary caregiver, if you are devastated, he will probably feel the blow. So if you were attached to the pet that died, you'll need to make sure that you take care of your own grieving and feelings of loss.

It's easy to underestimate the pain and sorrow pet owners experience when they lose a beloved companion. If you try to ignore or get over your feelings quickly, you may find yourself unable to respond to your infant's needs. Give yourself the time and space to express and work through your pain. Calling a close friend who understands your affection for your deceased pet might be a good idea.

The death of a pet and burial rituals are opportunities to practice saying "all gone" and "bye-bye." If your child is less than a year old, be prepared to accept that he won't have the intensity of emotion about this that you or an older child might have.

> *A case in point...*
>
> After our dog died, my eleven-month-old son, Eric, often wandered over to Skippy's bed in the kitchen, crawled up into it, and sat there, peacefully sucking his thumb. He seemed to sense that something was wrong. Whenever I saw him there, I would go over, pick him up, and say, "Skippy's all gone." Sometimes Eric stayed snugly in my arms, but other times he fidgeted until I put him down. Then he was off on a new adventure.

Toddlers

For children between twelve months and three years of age, the death of a pet can be more meaningful than for a baby, but toddlers still don't really understand the finality of death. Learning to separate from you is their major task. Their capacity to bond with a pet, while greater than that of a younger child, is still not strong enough to result in genuine grief.

Nevertheless, the experiences accumulated in an additional year or two of living have provided a toddler with lots more opportunities to become acquainted with loss, pets, and death. Like a hummingbird, a toddler darts here and there and never seems to light. He stays sad, too, only for short periods. Though he can't sustain attention on anything for long, greater mobility and language skills increase his ability to relate to a pet. Repetition is the way he learns. Even though he can't remember or understand everything that happens with the death of a pet, this event can be an important step in preparing him for bigger losses to come.

Preschoolers

For a preschooler, the death of a pet can be as serious and painful as if it were the death of a family member, and it's essential that you realize how sharply your child can feel the loss. Your openness and honesty about what happened to his pet is vital. His trust in you rides on your honesty with him, and once lost, a child's trust is hard to recover.

> *A case in point...*
>
> "Hi, Mommy! Where's Pepe?" Pauli asked when Pepe wasn't there to greet him after school.

I put my arm around him. "Sweetie, I have some very sad news to tell you," I said. "Right after you left for school, I heard car brakes squealing and went outside to see what was happening. Somehow, Pepe had gotten loose. He must have been running across the street. A car hit him. Pepe died."

"No! No!" Pauli pushed me away and ran from the room.

When I walked into the kitchen, Pauli was standing at the back door, tears steaming down his face, shouting desperately for Pepe to come. After a few minutes his sobs abated, and I picked him up and carried him into the family room. We sat down on the sofa, and I held him in my arms as we both cried for Pepe.

"Pepe was such a good dog," I said. "We all loved him very much. I feel sad right now. I know you do, too, Pauli. It hurts a lot when we lose a special friend."

It's very easy for a child to feel guilty and blame himself when his pet dies. This is particularly true when he was responsible for some or all of the pet's care. He needs you to help him interpret the facts. Tell him that everyone makes mistakes and that anyone could have left the gate open. Reassuring your child that the death wasn't his fault, repeating to help him understand what death means, and creating a ritual to allow him to name and validate his feelings are the most important things you can do to help him cope.

The death of a pet can provide an excellent opportunity to practice feeling talk. Your preschooler is still grappling with language, so repeating and stating facts in several different ways will help him understand such events and his feelings about them. Listening to his questions and answering them honestly gives you a rich opportunity to clarify his understanding of death and encourage good grieving.

Even if the dead animal wasn't a pet, you need to respect your preschooler's feelings. His need to understand and his questions will challenge you because of the literal way he thinks. Sometimes the greatest challenge will be for you to restrain your amusement. Even though you might find such questions amusing, you need to take them seriously—as they are intended.

A case in point...

One day at the beach, Jim's four-year-old son ran up to him, grabbed his hand, and led him to where a seagull lay dead in the sand.

"Daddy, what happened to him?" the boy asked.

"He died and went to heaven," Jim replied.

The youngster cocked his head pensively and asked, "Did God throw him back down?"

When your child's pet dies, some friends may advise you to get a new one quickly, but it's better to wait until he asks for one. It's always important to allow time for grieving after a loss. Otherwise, the message you send is, "Feeling sad is a bad thing. Get rid of those sad feelings as soon as you can." Such messages impoverish a child by cutting him off from a full emotional life. This in turn could affect his capacity for intimacy for a long time, perhaps for the rest of his life.

Power Points

- ✓ Be honest about what happened to your child's pet.
- ✓ Reassure him that the death was not his fault.
- ✓ Repeat to help him understand what death means.
- ✓ Create a burial ritual to allow him to name and validate his feelings.
- ✓ Allow time for grieving before getting a new pet.

Although death's permanence, irreversibility, and universality are entirely beyond the comprehension of a young child, including him in rituals to mark death transitions and talking about the deaths of insects, animals, and pets can be useful preparation for the future. Even though the child might not understand fully, discussions of this kind can help you practice talking about a subject that is largely taboo in our society.

A case in point...

As a young woman, I would take my children on nature walks. We played in dead leaves in the fall, smelled the blossoms in the spring, and watched insects, birds, and animals in the summer. But not until I had grandchildren did I realize what a rich opportunity these outings provided to teach young children about the cycle of life and death.

When my granddaughter Erica was eleven months old and just starting to walk, she waddled in her low-riding diaper along the park path looking at all the ants and bugs. Much closer to the ground than I was, she saw the world of insects better. Whenever she spotted a dead bug, she would squat down and look closely at it and touch it. After listening to her jabber on, describing her discovery, I'd say, "That little bug is dead. It doesn't move anymore."

As time went by and Erica became a big girl of a toddler, I added to her knowledge by answering her questions in a simple, direct way. "The bird can't eat because it is dead." As I slowly added the information she requested, she came to know that dead animals could not breathe, see, hear, or go to the bathroom, and she began to grasp the significance of this change.

One day we saw a dog that had been struck and killed by an automobile. Erica was curious, but also apprehensive. I answered her questions and responded to her obvious concern by saying, "The dog doesn't hurt anymore."

When Erica was two and a half, her kitten was run over and killed. This was another opportunity to help her understand and feel some of the sadness of death. Her mom and dad weren't afraid to cry as they held Erica and talked with her.

"It makes us sad," her mom said. "Hoot has been with us a long time, and it will be hard not to have him around anymore." Erica put her cheek on Hoot's fluffy body. However simply, her parents had helped her understand that this was an important event.

They held a simple funeral for Hoot. They wrapped him in a small blanket, put him in a nice box, and buried him in the backyard. Erica's father put a little cross on the grave, and her mother helped her plant a pansy over it.

Erica's grandfather died when she was six. It was a difficult time for everyone, but we were glad that Erica had experienced the deaths of leaves and bugs and animals, even of Hoot, before she had to cope with the loss of one of the most important adults in her life.

You would know the secret of death.
But how shall you find it unless you seek it in the heart of life?

KAHLIL GIBRAN

9

A Time to Weep

To weep is to make less the depth of grief.

Shakespeare

Before you can help a child grieve losses, you'll need to be familiar with the natural process of human grieving in adults. That's what this chapter is about. The more you understand the process of loss, grieving, and healing, the better able you'll be to prepare your children to handle the inevitable losses of life.

Grieving Your Losses

As an adult, you've lived long enough to become familiar with grieving—the normal reaction to any experience of loss. It occurs when a person acknowledges a loss and reacts emotionally to it. But although it is a natural reaction, it doesn't come naturally. Grieving skills are learned. Since the tendency in American culture is to suppress grieving, you might discover as you read that you haven't yet grieved some of your own losses.

One way our culture gets in the way of good grieving is by supporting idealized images of the self. In the face of grief, we consider it heroic and selfless to be "strong" for others. Yet all this does is stifle our thoughts and feelings. When you're grieving, you are being strong, because letting your grief out is hard work. It takes tremendous courage to tell someone about your feelings after a loss.

We also tend to believe that we will heal if we just "give it time." Time itself does not heal; healing comes from processing grief over time. When grief stays buried under the surface, only the symptoms are treated, and the unresolved grief has cumulative negative emotional consequences. It separates us from ourselves so that our minds and bodies are no longer in harmony.

Working through your grief is the first step in being able to accept, understand, and help your child cope with his. Children receive permission to grieve from adults, so before you can help them, you must give yourself permission to grieve your own losses.

Most likely you've suffered a major loss at some time in your life. Try to remember how you reacted. If you're like most people, you grieved a bit at a time and in several ways. At first it may have been impossible for you to believe what you were told, or even what you saw. Did you become numb and unable to feel the feelings you knew were inside you? When you were able to feel, did you find yourself feeling angry? Guilty that you hadn't done something to prevent the loss and make things come out all right?

Such feelings are natural and to some degree necessary. Feeling is healing. Experiencing the emotions of grief is the way we come to terms with our losses so that grief doesn't consume the rest of our lives. But as those feelings took less of your emotional energy, did you finally reach a point where you felt strong enough to move forward with your life? Did you find a way to integrate your memories of your loved one into your life after your loss?

Not everyone goes through all of these phases, or experiences them in the same order, but after a loss most people go through at least some of them.[14]

Distancing Reactions to Major Losses

Shock and denial are common initial reactions to the experience of loss. They are the ways your mind distances you from the pain until you are better able to deal with it.

Shock stalls other physical and emotional responses and protects you from the full force of your pain, giving you a cushion of time to let your loss sink in. Only then do you begin to feel your emotions in their fullness.

A case in point...

One year to the day after my mother was killed in a gun accident, I walked into my psychologist's office. I was frightened because I couldn't sleep and was having nightmares. My sister and brothers were angry with me because I had been so stoic and unemotional throughout our mother's hospitalization and funeral. I also thought there was something wrong with me because I couldn't cry. I felt like a bad person.

Unlike me, the rest of my family hadn't been at home

> at the time of the shooting accident. I actually witnessed it, and after talking with my psychologist, I came to understand that because of that, I had been in shock ever since. Only then was I finally able to let the tears of grief flow for my mother.

> *Grief is itself a medicine.*
>
> William Cowper

You may experience shock as withdrawal from your surroundings or as a general sense of physical and emotional numbness. Time seems to stand still, or to be passing more slowly than life in the regular world.

In *Bury Me with Soldiers,* C. Wayne Standiford describes his first major engagement as an eighteen-year-old soldier in Vietnam. Here's how he recalls his reaction to the death of his commanding officer, Lieutenant Crary:

> The corpsman was working in what seemed a frame-by-frame flurry of peculiar motions. The lieutenant still lay peaceful, much too peaceful. A chopper hovered overhead while another spread gunfire into the tree line. I was told to hustle out and help form a security perimeter for the landing chopper. The entire North Vietnamese Army could have been charging, and I would never have seen them. It was as if I'd somehow become detached from what was going on around me. I couldn't keep my eyes off the men who were carrying the sleeping lieutenant toward the chopper. I couldn't believe what I

> was seeing. I had no idea what his wounds were, but somehow I knew they were mortal. Frame by frame the movie rolled.
>
> The lieutenant was placed gently into the bowels of the bird. I didn't hear the blades hammer at the air as the chopper lifted off. I saw, but I didn't hear. "Red," our burly radioman went by me firing his .45 at our rear. More gunfire erupted up the line, but it seemed a distant, unimportant event. I stood frozen in my confusion.[15]

Sometimes, when faced with intense trauma, the mind walls off the painful event for a long period of time. This type of shock is called "dissociation." It's the mind's way of protecting your inner self from being overwhelmed by a sudden assault of unbearable pain. Standiford again:

> The next day there was a brief memorial service. The words of the chaplain sounded like a distant echo. There were three other rifles standing on their bayonets, but I didn't ask about the other men killed in action. I hadn't seen their bodies and hadn't even known about their deaths. They must have been killed on that same patrol, but I couldn't remember anything but the death of the lieutenant. I felt like a very old teenager with a jagged memory.
>
> The service seemed so futile, as if it had nothing to do with the man who had just died. Afterwards, someone said that the lieutenant had a wife and probably a baby by now. It was the last memorial I attended in Vietnam. Never again would I stand solemn in the church of combat. It was the evil one's first victory over my faith.[16]

Generally, the mind brings out these shielded facts and emotions later, when it can more readily deal with them. But when it forgets to do this, the grief hides away in a corner of the mind, out of conscious reach, until a tangential event causes the mind to recall and process the grief.

A case in point...

On a bombing mission over Germany, my friend's plane, flying on my right wing, exploded in flames and went down. I had little time to think of my friend or feel grief. I had mission after mission to complete.

Five years later, I thought I saw my friend enter Saks in downtown Chicago. I ran to catch up with him, grabbed him by the shoulder, and shouted, "Joe!" A total stranger turned, looked at me with a mixture of apprehension and confusion, then walked on. I wept. Finally, I began to grieve my friend's death.

When repressed grief emerges, your mind and feelings can deal with it. But if it isn't recalled and processed, it can cause problems in your physical, mental, and spiritual life, as well as in relationships with others. Standiford put it this way: "I needed water for my soul, but death stood between me and the well."[17]

Like shock, denial can keep you from having to adapt too quickly to a loss that results in more pain than you can handle all at once. Denial, or the refusal or inability to believe that something has happened, allows you to distance yourself from facts and feelings so you can take them in more gradually.

Standiford sums up the experience of many soldiers who watched their friends die in the Vietnamese War: "Something in our young minds seemed to block ordinary grief, like a water pump that seizes up and doesn't get the water out of the well. After each incident, we just went about our business. We had become experts of denial."[18] As with shock, if denial continues unrelieved, what is initially a protective biological response can become a serious disturbance that prevents you from moving on with life.

Shock and denial often manifest themselves in gallows humor. Police officers, emergency response teams, military personnel in combat, and physicians report times when, in the midst of severe crises and horrible losses, they find themselves telling dark or silly jokes, laughing uproariously over inappropriate things, little things, or nothing, even when they are acutely aware of what is happening. The laughter is a kind of substitute for tears, a releasing of a different emotion that can provide healing during painful episodes where neither complete denial nor shock is a likely recourse. This can also occur in everyday situations.

A case in point...

After a long week of grieving for and burying our brother, my sister and I were cleaning up after dinner. For no apparent reason, everything we said and did made us laugh. Washing the dishes together, gathering wood for the fire, or helping one of the children tie his shoelaces elicited strangely healing, emotionally cleansing peals of laughter.

Although the difficulty of change and the pain of loss seem to give us little reason for mirth, laughing in the midst of our pain can help us through the grieving process.

> *Laugh out loud. It helps flush out the nervous system.*
>
> CHARLES SWINDOLL

PERSONALIZING REACTIONS TO MAJOR LOSSES

In addition to "distancing" reactions like shock and denial, there are also "personalizing" reactions to major losses. As shock and denial pass and the reality of the loss begins to sink in, the feelings that most commonly arise are sadness, anger, and guilt.

Perhaps the most common feeling response to loss of all kinds—illness, accident, separation, or death—is sadness. Because each human being is unique, we don't all feel sadness alike, and we express it in many different ways. The most obvious indication of sadness is crying, but not all people cry when they're sad, and crying doesn't necessarily mean that a person is sad.

Tears after a loss, however, are a pretty fair indication of sadness. Crying is one of the ways we express and release painful or pent up feelings. Like humor, tears can be healing. In *Lessons I Learned in the Dark,* Jennifer Rothschild says that she had to learn that crying is a good thing:

> I think that I had to learn to cry because I misunderstood the purpose of tears. For a long time I mistakenly assumed

> that the weight of tears would undermine my strength. You've heard the expression "reduced to tears." It makes it sound as though crying is the final, most debasing result of sorrow, as if our tears weaken us and make us smaller.
>
> But that's not true....
>
> Crying never washes away hope into an ocean of despair; it helps cleanse the eyes of our souls so we can more clearly see the source of our hope. [19]

Trying to make sense of life after a major loss, people often feel angry and look for someone or something to blame. Personalizing and directing anger is your mind's way of trying to rationally come to terms with your feelings. One person might feel angry with God for having taken a life or for allowing pain and hardship. Another might feel angry with a doctor or hospital for not saving a life or preventing the catastrophic consequences of an injury. Yet another might feel anger toward the person who has died.

A case in point...

Following the death of my uncle, my aunt was having a rotten day. A pile of business and legal documents needed to be filled out, but she couldn't find her husband's records. That was the last straw.

"Damn you, Henry!" she screamed. "Why did you die and leave me with all this?"

Then she burst into tears.

Anger in itself isn't a bad emotion. It's a legitimate response to certain situations. The way we express that emotion, however, can be good or bad. Channeling loss-related anger into constructive activities is not only healthy for the person expressing it, but it can also be beneficial for society as a whole. For example, after a drunk driver killed her daughter, an angry mother founded Mothers Against Drunk Drivers (MADD).

Guilt is another common emotional reaction to loss. "If only I had!" "If only I hadn't!" That's what my brother felt after Raymond was killed when the tractor he was driving skidded off a bridge. He felt responsible for Raymond's death, guilty that he had not taken the tractor out that morning. In truth, the day before the fatal accident, he had injured his left arm fixing the combine, and the doctor had advised him to stay off the tractor for several days. Nevertheless, he was overwhelmed with guilt, unable to shake the thought that if only he had driven the tractor, Raymond would still be alive.

As with anger and blame, guilt seems to stem from the human craving to understand why suffering occurs. Whatever the loss, those suffering it struggle to make sense of it. Through guilt, the person takes on personal responsibility for what has happened. To a person who isn't grieving, this appears far from rational, but for the bereaved, guilt provides the illusion of logic and understanding, if only for a short time.

After a loss, you may feel out of sync with others and the world. I remember that a week after I returned home from caring for my father for several weeks, my brother called to tell me that Dad had died. My sister and I flew to South Dakota from California, hooking up with my brother in Salt Lake City. On the plane, my brother and sister chatted away, but all I could do was look out the window, tears streaming down my face. Though I was not alone, I felt lonely, isolated, cut off from my brother and sister by my own feelings.

When grief is overwhelming, it can lead to changes in eating and sleeping patterns, sometimes accompanied by changes in weight. Recalling the final stages of her mother's fight against ovarian cancer, Laurel Brunvoll writes:

> The first week after I became one of my mom's primary caregivers, I lost more than ten pounds. Food had lost its taste, and with it went my desire to eat. When my mom could no longer eat anything, I started skipping meals even more frequently.... One person asked, "What good can you be to your mom if you starve yourself to death?" Those were harsh words, but they woke me up to what I was doing. For a long time I ate not because I felt like it, but because I knew I had to.[20]

Stressing the importance of self-care in times of loss, Laurel encourages people who find themselves exhibiting extreme behavior patterns to seek professional help.

Such personalizing reactions are normal during acute grief. But if you remain caught up in one of them, your quality of life can be seriously diminished. A person who doesn't pass through the phase of anger can become intolerant and bitter; an individual who doesn't move beyond guilt or sadness can suffer depression.

It's important to recognize when grief has incapacitated you. If you have any of these symptoms, you might need to seek professional help with the grieving process:

- suffering from unresolved guilt that goes beyond feeling guilty about what you did or didn't do at the time of the loss;
- thinking about killing or hurting yourself, or doing things that place you in danger of being hurt or killed;

- constantly telling yourself that you are worthless or bad;
- finding it nearly impossible to get moving in the morning or to go anywhere;
- having ongoing problems getting work or schoolwork completed or taking care of your responsibilities at home;
- experiencing visions or hearing voices or sounds not associated with the loss.

Coping Reactions to Major Losses

As bereaved people work through the pain of the grieving process, the initial shock and denial fade, and sad, angry, and guilty feelings occur less frequently, less intensely, and for shorter periods of time. They learn to live with their unanswered questions, realize they will survive the loss, and begin again to live in the present and look to the future. Their sense of humor and energy return, and they surge into life again. Although it may take some people many years, they finally reach the stage where they accept the feelings they have experienced.

Recently we have come to understand that, for many people, acceptance doesn't mean accepting the end of a relationship with the person who has died, but rather integrating that relationship into their lives in a new way.

A case in point...

My sister's baby daughter died at one month of age. The first year was very difficult for my sister, but her one-year-old son kept her focused on life. Over the years, I knew that she still thought about her daughter frequently, especially on the anniversaries of her birth and death.

It wasn't until the death of one of her good friends many years later that my sister shared that she has an ongoing relationship with her daughter. She often finds her in her dreams and talks with her. Over the years this baby has grown into a young woman. In my sister's most recent dream, her daughter was walking on the beach with her friend, and they were at peace.

Nearly thirty years after he left Vietnam, C. Wayne Standiford met Lieutenant Crary's widow:

> I was at loss for words and choking up a bit. I kicked myself for not bringing a handkerchief. I wanted this woman to know that her husband's men had held him in the highest regard on the battlefield, and I tried to convey to her how defining my short meeting with him had been. I told her that when he was wounded, extreme efforts were made to protect him from further harm. Everything was done to try to save him.
>
> As I wound up the story of my first patrol, I wanted to stand up and give her a full salute. But I didn't think either of us could cope with the emotions that deep gesture of respect would unleash. Both of us held ourselves together, but our runny noses and weeping eyes kept me running back and forth to the sink to fetch some rough old paper towels. [21]

Wayne's recollection of the meeting shows that he had at last accepted the loss of Lieutenant Crary, who for him was symbolic of all the courageous men who died in the war. Focusing on the honor with which they served allowed him to integrate the loss into his life and enabled his pump to begin flowing again.

In adults the grieving process is most clearly evident in a major loss such as death, but the process is the same for any loss. The process in children, while sharing many of the same characteristics, depends on the loss itself and the developmental stage at which it occurs. The more you know about both grieving and your child's developmental needs, the better able you'll be to help him through all his losses.

Power Points

- ✓ Learn about the grieving process.
- ✓ Give yourself permission to grieve your losses.
- ✓ Understand your child's developmental needs.

Weeping may remain for a night,
but rejoicing comes in the morning.

Psalm 30:5

10

Bereaved Babies

Oh, fear not in a world like this
And thou shall know ere long,
Know how sublime a thing it is
To suffer and be strong.

Henry Wadsworth Longfellow

The most devastating loss imaginable for a young child is the death of a primary caregiver. No matter how prepared a child is, losing a loved one will be deeply painful to him. The word from which *bereaved* is derived means "robbed," and that's just how a young child feels—robbed of a valued and necessary part of his life.

How a child grieves the loss depends on a number of factors, including his attachment to the caregiver, the suddenness of the loss, the degree of disruption of his daily activities, and the availability of people to support him. The depth of his grief will depend on what the loss means to him, and that in turn depends on his age, his capacity to understand what has happened, and to what extent his caregivers have used previous experiences as opportunities to help him grow and gain through losses.

Grieving Infants

An infant has no sense of time and cannot know that a caregiver is "all gone." To the degree he is aware of the loss, however, your baby will be as overwhelmed as any adult would be by the death of a loved one.

The term caregiver—rather than parent, father, or mother—is appropriate for this developmental stage because during the first year of life, actions define relationships. An infant is aware of the person who consistently feeds, changes, bathes, and comforts him. If a father who wasn't regularly engaged in these activities were to die, his baby might not even be aware that he was no longer there. In such a case, if you are the baby's primary caregiver, your response to the loss will determine how he reacts. Though he isn't capable of understanding that death is irreversible, he is aware of your nonverbal messages and acutely sensitive to your emotional reactions to the loss.

If you are pained by an external thing,
it is not this thing that disturbs you—
but your judgment about it.

MARCUS AURELIUS

Some reactions to loss involve mental processes that your infant hasn't yet developed. For example, denial and guilt cannot help him process grief until he is about four years old. An infant can, however, express his grief through sadness, anger, and shock. He might reveal his sadness by persistent fussiness or inconsolable crying, or signal his anger by screaming at the top of his lungs and refusing to be calmed. Shock is rare in an infant, but when it does occur, it is life threatening and requires immediate professional attention.

A case in point...

When my son Joshua was six months old and still nursing, my wife was killed in a car accident. In fact, she was nursing him in the car when the accident occurred. Afterward, he refused to eat or drink for a week and had to be fed intravenously. He stopped exploring his world and was sad and withdrawn for several weeks. The only thing he seemed to want was for me to hold him. It took considerable love and patience to draw him out of the numbness and withdrawal of shock and back into the world.

As with Joshua, your baby might grieve in physical ways. Extreme distress is most common during the first three days after a loss, but the stress of bereavement can compromise your infant's immune system and leave him vulnerable to a variety of physical disorders. He may get more colds and ear infections or have bouts of constipation or diarrhea. He might have problems sleeping or eating. Because he is so small, weight loss can be life threatening and must be monitored.

A death in the family naturally upsets a baby's schedule. If his mother has died, he may cry angrily for her, throw himself about, shake or rock in his crib, or look eagerly for any sight or sound that might prove to be his missing mother. Intermittent spells of crying could continue for a week or more. It will be especially difficult for a baby who has been breast-feeding if his mother's milk dries up as a result of the loss, or if his mother dies. In such circumstances, the baby may not be able to accept soothing, and he will need lots of opportunities to suck to help him self-soothe.

In his need for security, reassurance, and soothing, your baby might become whiny and clingy. If he has already started being weaned or toilet trained, there's a good chance he will regress in these areas. If he has begun to walk, he might revert to crawling or want to be carried more. His anguish might be particularly evident at bedtime and during the night. Although nightmares are neither common nor uncommon at this age, the stress and anxiety of those around him may cause him to have more bad dreams.

The death of a spouse is particularly difficult for the surviving mate to handle. If you are that person, the death will place immense demands on you. Not only must you do whatever you can to help your child cope, but you also have to work through your own loss. If it has left you devastated and depleted, you might not have enough physical and emotional resources to adequately support your baby. This doesn't mean you shouldn't grieve—even if it were possible to stop yourself from doing so. It means that if you feel you aren't emotionally stable and available to your baby, you need to lean heavily on your support system to soothe your baby when you cannot.

In many cases, the surviving parent simply isn't able to provide for the baby's needs immediately after the death. If that's the case, a competent caregiver must be found. This could be a family member whose grief is not incapacitating, or another warm, understanding, responsible person, preferably someone the baby already knows, who can be with him all day and give him the care, support, and nurturing he needs.

If you feel emotionally out of control—and mourning can cause overwhelming distress in anyone—you need to let someone else care for your child. Your baby can handle your sadness, but anger or unmanageable feelings of any kind are challenging, and even emotionally damaging, for him. And if your grieving interferes too long with resuming your normal activities, you might need to seek professional help. Your infant is likely to suffer ill effects if you, his primary caregiver, are withdrawn for long periods of time. The only way you can help him is to take care of yourself first. Otherwise, your bereaved child effectively loses two caregivers.

Even with the best of care, your baby may feel intense anguish as he experiences this loss. If you suddenly find yourself his primary caregiver, adapting your schedule to the nurturing routine he is used to will help support him and make the adjustment easier. This involves paying prompt and affectionate attention to his needs and maintaining the sleeping and eating schedule he has been used to. This transition time will be easier if the deceased caregiver has left a written account of the child's activities, habits, and how he was disciplined. Knowing his likes and dislikes, daily schedule and routines, and favorite games and toys will enable you to keep things as normal as possible for him.

Mourning Toddlers

An eighteen-month-old baby understands more about what death means than an infant does, but he still can't comprehend it as a final and irreversible event. Although he's beginning to use words, his understanding is rudimentary, and he can't use language to process his experiences. He tends to understand descriptions about things and actions only in context of the here and now, so "all gone" is still relative and reversible in his mind. However, he does know when someone who is supposed to be there is not, particularly when that person is his primary caregiver, and he will grieve the loss.

> *Alone! That worn-out word, so idly spoken, and so coldly heard. Yet all that poets sing and grief hath known of hopes laid waste, knells on that word—Alone!*
>
> EDWARD BULWER-LYTTON

As with the surviving parent of an infant, a toddler's caregiver must first take care of himself so that the toddler will not effectively suffer a double loss. And just like an infant, your toddler will react to the new situation by checking out your responses. If you are overwrought, he will feel your anguish and probably signal his misery by loud and persistent crying.

If you can tolerate his signals of distress and are able to hold and comfort him, doing so will be healing for both of you. If you aren't able to do that, it would be better to leave him in the hands of another competent and nurturing caregiver. Otherwise, his primary attachment could be jeopardized. That, in turn, could create the need for professional assistance to prevent serious long-term emotional wounds.

If the attachment is not threatened but the baby's life is disrupted, you'll know he's distressed if he cries or whines more than usual, doesn't respond to soothing as he usually does, changes his eating or sleeping patterns, or has more frequent or intense tantrums. All of these reactions are signals that your baby needs all the sensitive response you can provide him, both from within yourself and from other trusted adults.

Your child's eating and sleeping patterns might be disturbed. Offer him a variety of nutritious fluids and foods, and allow him to choose what appeals to him. Be flexible in meeting his nutritional needs, and don't force him to eat. Night fears can be a problem for a child of this age, and he might insist on sleeping with you or a sibling at night. Giving him a warm bath and an oil body massage will help relax him. Be sure he has his favorite blanket or teddy bear. Read him his favorite story and nestle him in for sleep. If he has a bad dream, he may need twenty minutes or more of cuddling and soft reassuring talk before he'll be able to go back to sleep.

Your toddler is learning short sentences, some of which are assertive or contrary. He is still egocentric and thinks everything revolves around him. You are likely to hear the word *no* more and see more stubbornness. He will want things to be the way he wants them to be regardless of what you say or how well you handle things. This little person's affection for you can warm your heart, but he can also show ownership by jealousy. Hyperactivity and aggressive behavior toward peers or adults are also common. He will need your patience and sensitivity as well as extra time and attention from you.

A grieving toddler may experience a range of emotions, including shock, anger, and sadness bordering on despair. How he expresses his feelings will depend on his level of cognitive development and verbal fluency. A shock reaction in a child this age might involve withdrawing from activities he previously enjoyed, reverting to behaviors like thumb-sucking, or reversing the progress he has made in weaning or toilet training. The most common reactions to loss in this age group, however, are sadness and anger.

Your baby might indicate that he feels sad through frequent clinging, sobbing fits, and episodes of flailing in his crib. Expecting the return of the loved one, he may repeatedly look toward the door, and then crumple up his little face and burst into sobs of distress. As this is the stage of the "terrible twos," world-class tantrums are most likely manifestations of angry feelings, even though what triggers them may not appear to be directly related to the loss. The signals a toddler sends during this transition don't seem to relate clearly to any particular event. For example, for no apparent reason, he may burst into tears right before eating.

When a toddler has a tantrum in response to his primary caregiver's death, the surviving caregiver will need great emotional strength to remain calm. The toddler has no idea what's wrong, and shaking, hitting, or spanking him will only make him feel scared, confused, and even angrier. As both his neediness and his caregiver's need to respond escalate, the situation can quickly spiral out of control.

Clear, consistent discipline is necessary at this time, and you must be able to say, "No, you cannot go into the street. A car might hit you. If you try to go into the street, you will have to sit in your chair." When there's a lot of pain in a home, maintaining loving discipline is difficult, yet what your toddler needs most is a caregiver who is consistent and in control and sets reasonable limits.

A toddler's anger might be related to the loss, but it might also be related to how you are coping with it. He is more likely to misunderstand silent sorrow than open mourning. If you withdraw in sadness, a toddler will feel the barrier created if you don't communicate with him in your usual manner. On the other hand, your toddler can tolerate and even benefit from your tears.

A case in point…

In the days after my wife died, I would sometimes sit in my chair with tears streaming down my face. Seeing me, my twenty-month-old son Frank would say, "Daddy cry?"

I knew he needed to be reassured, so I would pick him up and cradle him in my lap and say, "Yes, sweetie, Daddy's

> crying. I'm missing Mama a lot, and I feel very sad. This is a sad time for both of us."
>
> I didn't want to hide my real feelings from my son. I wanted him to learn that it's okay to feel sad and that crying is okay, too.

If a baby's mother has died and the father is able to parent, he can provide his toddler with the best care by participating in whatever cultural and religious rituals are meaningful and thus healing for him, engaging actively in the mourning process, and giving himself and his child permission to grieve. This self-care will enhance his ability to provide his toddler with plenty of quality time and soothing.

Until he has recovered from the loss of his mother, a toddler may experience intense separation anxiety whenever his father or other caregiver leaves him. The caregiver must understand what the baby is signaling and be able to give him the extra attention and soothing he needs. If at all possible, have friends and family come to your home to help instead of taking your child to them. Keeping changes to a minimum gives your bereaved youngster a chance to adjust. He is bewildered enough without any additional changes.

The awareness that one of his parents has disappeared will trigger your toddler's fear that you will, too. He might become extra clingy and even refuse to have you out of his sight. He needs reassurance. Negotiate separations gently and give him clear reassurances that you love him and will return. It will help if you arrange your schedule to allow extra time to be with him before you leave for work—time to hold him, to play with him, and to tell him "I love you" and "Daddy will be home after work."

> *The knowledge that we are never alone calms the troubled sea of our lives and speaks peace to our souls.*
>
> A. W. Tozer

There may be times when you need to be away from your toddler to meet your own emotional needs and process your own grief. At such times, it's important to have another caregiver who is able to help your toddler express his feelings, to answer his questions, to give him all the comforting he needs, and to assure him that you love him and will be back. The most effective form of reassurance depends on his age and verbal skills. If he can talk, words work best, followed by hugs and other nonverbal soothing.

Parents often worry about how to answer their toddler's questions. Don't be surprised if he asks the same questions over and over. A toddler's repetitive and seemingly endless questions are most likely indications of his confusion and grief. Look at them as opportunities to provide clarifying and reassuring information—even if he asks you the same question forty-six times. When a toddler signals his distress through questions like these, it means that he has much to learn and is working hard at doing so.

A case in point...

The day my daughter died, my son-in-law brought my granddaughter, Olivia, to stay with me while he made arrangements for the funeral.

When I took her in my arms, Olivia began asking questions. "Where is Mommy now?" "Is she coming home for dinner?" "Will she come kiss me good night?" "When will I see Mommy again?" "Will my daddy die, too?"

As her verbal skills were quite well developed, she knew and thought she understood the word *dead*. But she really couldn't process the word in relation to her mother.

A sensitive response to such questions means giving a toddler simple, direct answers he can understand. "There was an accident and Mommy died" or "Mommy died of a disease called cancer." Don't say too much. Answer only the questions he asks, and watch him carefully to see how much information he can handle. Remember that he is still building a trusting relationship with you, and answer his questions as honestly as you can. If you don't know the answer to a question, tell him so and try to find the answer with him.

Caregivers who respond sensitively to these cues can do a wonderful job of teaching a bereaved child how to cope with loss by talking about his feelings and holding and soothing him as he expresses them. Whatever he is feeling, reassure him that his feelings are normal and that he is loved.

Power Points

- ✓ Give your child and yourself lots of TLC.
- ✓ When you talk or play with your child, do it at eye level.
- ✓ Speak to your child in a soft, soothing tone of voice.
- ✓ Tolerate emotional and developmental regression.
- ✓ Set clear and consistent limits.
- ✓ Give your support system opportunities to help you and your child.

The loss of a baby's primary attachment figure to death is a traumatic event characterized by intense deprivation and disorientation. Good grieving depends a great deal on the availability of a nurturing caregiver who can provide for his physical and emotional needs, give him physical and verbal reassurances that he is safe and being taken of, and help allay his fear of further loss.

If you are called upon to support a baby after the death of his primary caregiver, remember that it is impossible for you to be perfectly sensitive in your responses to him, especially if his loss is also yours. No parent can be perfect, and fortunately, being perfect isn't necessary. Even excellent parenting isn't required. Good-enough parenting is all human beings can realistically achieve, and when it's based on love, it works well through good and bad times alike.

Seek Love in the pity of others' woe, in the gentle relief of another's care, in the darkness of night and winter's snow, with the naked and outcast—See Love there.

WILLIAM BLAKE

11

No Road Back

There are things in life which are irreparable;
there is no road back to yesterday.

Oswald Chambers

The death of a primary caregiver is devastating for a preschooler. While he may not yet fully understand the irreversibility and permanence of death, he can ignore neither the fact that his mother or father is gone nor the emotional reactions of those around him.

Magical Language

Between the ages of three and five, a child uses language in a way he could not when he was younger. He can ask for and understand verbal descriptions of what is going on around him. He is apt to persistently demand to know "why" and can understand many of the responses he is given. He has verbal memories of what has happened.

But while his language skill is becoming increasingly sophisticated, by adult standards his thinking is illogical and irrational. For a preschooler, magic is everywhere, and it's real for him. He develops wonderful fantasies in which he can place his faith and may believe that he can destroy the world and then restore the dead to life. He has yet to learn that death is irreversible.

A child at this age tends to view the world as revolving around him. Although he is still egocentric, he's not selfish in the same way a toddler is. Self-control and initiative are becoming important to him. He is aware of right and wrong and places value on praise and punishment. At this developmental stage, his task is to develop a sense that he is able to impact his world, as well as the people in it.

This can get complicated when a major loss occurs. The rich fantasy life of a child at this age can backfire by contributing to inappropriate feelings of culpability. As your child approaches the age of five, he might display reactions that suggest he has feelings of guilt. For example, if his father dies, he may recall a time when he wished Daddy would "just disappear." That leads him to conclude that he caused the death. Magical thinking—a cognitive process that makes him think he can wish things away and that his wish will be granted—can persuade him that he is responsible for the tragedy. Consequently, he may be overwhelmed by guilt and see the loss as a punishment for wrongdoing. He might also misunderstand the grief reactions of adults around him and perceive them as disappointment with or anger at him.

> *The home where happiness securely dwells was never wrought by charms and magic spells.*
>
> ARTHUR WALLACE PEACH

Magical thinking does not happily coincide with reality, and you must patiently, persistently, and lovingly contradict unrealistic feelings of responsibility. If your child feels guilty, sadness and tears are likely to alternate with despair. As with lesser losses, these experiences provide opportunities for you to allow, name, accept, and validate feelings within the context of verbal and physical reassurances that the death was not his fault.

Like infants and toddlers, a preschooler is likely to feel sad and angry, and he may experience shock. He may express sadness through frequent bouts of crying, difficulty in falling or staying asleep, and nightmares. Nightmares are common at this age anyway because of the development of language and a fantasy life, but grief and trauma can make the nightmares more intense. Although he won't remember his night terrors, they will be obvious to you when he cries, yells, or tries to walk, run, or fight in his sleep. Night terrors may indicate that he's having a very hard time expressing some deep feelings and fears.

Physical reactions to a major loss may include loss of appetite, weight loss or failure to gain weight at expected rates, and gastrointestinal problems such as constipation or diarrhea. As with bereaved people of all ages, heartaches can manifest themselves as body aches. Stress can depress your child's immune system, making him more vulnerable to infections or other physical disorders. Most likely he will engage in behaviors that were typical of him at a younger age, such as clinging, thumb-sucking, and bed-wetting.

Your preschooler may express anger through physical outbursts against parents, siblings, peers, and pets. He may become upset more quickly and throw tantrums, much as he once did as a toddler, and might display shock by withdrawing from ordinary activities such as favorite games or pastimes. Emotional numbing may be evident in inappropriate repetitive questioning. Moreover, the answers might have no perceptible effect on him.

In addition, he is able to react with denial, and he may use imaginative storytelling to deny the truth of the loss. What to you may appear to be lies are really his way of protecting himself and trying to make sense of a painful event. To help him work through his grief, provide him with opportunities for exercise and imaginative play. Play with him. It will help you work through your grief, too.

An imaginary friend, a common occurrence at this stage, may develop in response to the death of a primary caregiver. Creating a playmate over whom he has total control and with whom he can practice interacting provides a preschooler with an excellent tool for coping. The film *Bogus* shows how a child creates an imaginary friend to deal with his intense grief after the death of his mother. Adults in his life try to persuade him that Bogus doesn't exist, but their attempts are futile. He simply clings more tightly to Bogus.

It's probably best for you to accept your child's fantasy without making too big a deal of it. When the problem for which the imaginary friend was created has been resolved, he will disappear. In the film, it is only when the bereaved child's appointed guardian becomes his loving caregiver that he is able to give up Bogus.

Parents are inevitably their children's models. The old saying that actions speak louder than words has become trite precisely because it's true. How parents handle their grief is a far more powerful teacher than what they tell their children about grieving.

> *Children have never been very good at listening to their elders, but they have never failed to imitate them.*
>
> JAMES BALDWIN

A case in point...

My five-year-old son, Joey, helped care for his terminally ill father, which created a close bond between them. As the time of my husband's death drew nearer, I noticed that Joey was keeping his feelings inside.

"It's okay to cry when you feel sad about Daddy's not getting well," I said to him.

Joey didn't respond to this, so I repeated similar messages during the weeks that followed.

Finally one day Joey said, "Mommy, how come you don't cry?"

I was telling Joey that it was okay to cry, but by holding back my own tears, I was showing him that it was not.

For most of us, tears are a normal and healthful part of grieving—a release for sadness and pent-up feelings, a healthy outlet to relieve the stress of strong feelings. There are, however, some people who do not cry. Forcing tears if they don't come naturally is just as harmful as stifling them when you feel like crying. Remember that you're still developing a trusting relationship with your child and that your success depends upon your being honest with him.

While it is important to teach your child that death is natural part of life, not some fearful secret, whether or not he participates in a funeral depends in part on his level of maturity, the immediate situation, cultural traditions, and his preferences if he is old enough to communicate them. It is ill advised to force a child to participate in a viewing or funeral or any kind of ritual.

If your child does attend the funeral, you could ask an emotionally grounded, understanding caregiver to care for him and answer his questions in a simple and honest way while you attend to your own grieving and receive the condolences of family and friends. If he doesn't attend the funeral, you could leave him at home with an empathic caregiver. Later you might want to create the opportunity for a private service that will be meaningful to him. Another option is to videotape the ceremony and save it to give him when he is older as a parting gift from the loved one who has died.

If your preschooler wants to communicate with the caregiver he misses, suggest ways he can do this. He could draw pictures or write a letter expressing his feelings of loss and grief. He might want to put the letter in the casket. You can also support him by giving your support system opportunities to help both you and him. Inform his friends and teachers about his loss and help him figure out what to say to them when he returns to school.

> *Openness is to wholeness as secrets are to sickness.*
>
> BARBARA JOHNSON

SIGNS OF HEALTHY ADJUSTMENT

Successful resolution of your child's grieving is almost entirely dependent on the availability of a nurturing caregiver who can provide for his physical and emotional needs. At each stage of development, there are signs to let you know when he is coping successfully with a major loss.

An infant's emotional responses will even out, and his problems with eating and sleeping will decrease. He will have fewer health problems and more interest in exploring his world. Your toddler's successful coping is evident when he stops searching for the loved one, his energy returns, and he begins to participate in and enjoy playtime activities. He may begin to try to master potty training or give up thumb-sucking, and his tantrums will no longer be world class—just "toddler class."

As with infants and toddlers, you'll know that your preschooler is coping successfully when the problems that emerged during the grieving process subside. He will again enjoy normal activities and will be able to talk about sad and happy feelings, including his feelings about the loss he has experienced. He may use play activities to reenact and work through his experience.

A bereaved youngster needs time to heal and bond with a new mother or father figure. When your child begins to transfer his love to another person, recovery is well on its way. Here are some signs that a bereaved child is recovering:

- His crying, sleeping, and eating patterns return to normal.
- He resumes his developmental progress.
- His attention span increases.
- He isn't so clingy, and he feels more relaxed with others.
- He enjoys touches and hugs, and he is bonding with significant others.
- He is again a happy, responsive child.

If these indicators don't appear within a reasonable time—if he remains angry or gets into more than normal trouble, if night terrors persist, if denial and lies form new patterns of behavior—your child is signaling that he needs additional support and perhaps professional help. Responding to these signals can make all the difference in the world to your child's long-term emotional, mental, and physical well-being.

Power Points

- ✓ Contradict your child's unrealistic feelings of responsibility.
- ✓ Provide opportunities for exercise and imaginative play.
- ✓ Remember the lost loved one in meaningful ways on special occasions.
- ✓ Be honest about your own feelings.
- ✓ Remember that good-enough parenting truly is good enough.

To live in this world you must be able to do
three things: to love what is mortal,
to hold it against your bones knowing your
own life depends on it, and, when the time
comes to let it go, to let it go.

MARY OLIVER

12

It's about More than Death

They are not wrapped as gifts
(there was no time to wrap them),
but you will find them under the lighted tree
with the other presents.
They are the extra gifts, the ones with the hard names.

E. B. White

Major losses that affect a young child directly are few but crushing. Death is certainly one of them, but it's not the only one. Other devastating events that you hope he won't have to confront are divorce and disasters, either environmental or man-made. You cannot—no one can—ensure that he won't experience such tragic events. It is in part because of this that all the effort you make to learn the skills, acquire the knowledge, and teach your children good grieving is worth the time, energy, and love you commit to it.

When a child sustains a major loss, he feels less safe and secure.

As with the loss of a primary caregiver, a major catastrophe will cause him to be anxious about who will take care of him. For him, the issue is one of survival. And as with normal and common losses, what is at stake are his feelings and the ways you can help him acknowledge and grow from them at the different developmental levels.

> *Out of this nettle, danger, we pluck this flower, safety.*
>
> SHAKESPEARE

DIVORCE

Divorce, like death, is an event that rips through the fabric of a family's life. A number of factors contribute to the toll it takes on a family and the feeling of loss everyone in the family experiences. For parents who become primary caregivers, inadequate income and an increased workload often become major problems. For noncustodial parents whose contact with their children is less than they would like, there is a tremendous sense of loss. Whether they have custody or not, divorced single parents lack the emotional support of a partner, and despite the prevalence of divorce, our society is not supportive of divorced single-parent families.

A child's reactions to his parents' divorce are very similar to his reactions to the death of a parent, and so are his strategies for coping with the loss. The specific strategies suggested in chapters 10 and 11 for helping children who suffer the death of a caregiver are also effective for those experiencing parental divorce.

As with every other loss, an infant's reaction depends almost wholly on how his parents handle the divorce. Most crucial is the response of the parent with whom the baby is more closely bonded. If this parent manages to get through the experience of divorce without disrupting the baby's schedule too much, the infant is likely to remain relatively unscathed. Closer to one year of age, the baby is far more likely to recognize that a parent has left and experience that loss directly, and in contrast to an infant, a toddler is more likely to be affected by divorce, particularly if it changes the frequency or duration of contact with either parent. The question "Who will take care of me?" becomes the central issue of his life.

Much more verbal and mobile than younger children, your preschooler is also more aware of the conflicts in his family. He may even have drawn his own conclusions about what's happening before you talk with him. As I've already pointed out, children in this age group are notoriously susceptible to magical thinking, and it may be a harsh discovery for your preschooler that he cannot wish away your decision.

Also remember that a preschooler is likely to react to this loss with feelings of guilt. A preschooler's tendency to blame himself is so powerful that, after years of effort, the TV series Sesame Street finally gave up trying to create a segment from which children could learn that divorce is never their fault. No matter how they presented it, children polled after watching it were still convinced that the divorce was their fault. This means you might have to repeatedly clarify the distinction between feeling sad and feeling responsible.

Breaking the bond of marriage is an emotionally charged process, often loaded with conflict and lacking constructive communication. Parents' feelings can be so fragile that it can be difficult for them to reach out and support their children. The single most important way to help your child survive divorce is to take care of your own needs, because only then can you minimize the inevitable disruptions in his life. If you are healthy, rested, and emotionally stable, you will have the strength to keep his routine as normal as possible and to give him extra time, affection, and physical contact. A depleted parent has nothing to give. What matters most to the child's health and welfare is that his parents have the strength and composure to carry on despite their pain.

> ### *A case in point...*
>
> I was devastated when I realized that in not knowing how to heal myself, I had failed my family. If I had taken better care of myself at the time of my divorce, I would have healed faster. I wasn't able to express my feelings and needs or to reach out to people in my support system. Along with my work, I needed enjoyable exercise like swimming and tennis, adequate rest, more outings and vacations, and counseling to ease my depression.
>
> Because I didn't know then what I know now, I didn't do the things that would have supported my healing so that I, in turn, could support my family. It was difficult—almost impossible, really—to help my children in their grief when I hadn't first taken care of myself.

When parents are chronically troubled, their needs can override the developmental needs of children, and if there is no other adult who can take charge, the burden falls almost entirely on the child, usually the oldest.

A case in point...

I was five years old when my parents got a divorce. I remember the judge asking me who I wanted to live with, although I don't remember what I told him. The next thing I remember is standing next to my three-year-old sister, suitcase in hand, waiting for the Greyhound bus to take us somewhere. Before the bus arrived, I was told that I was now the "little man" of the family and that I needed to take care of my sister. I puffed out my chest and stood tall, but inside fear had my stomach in knots.

Such responsibility is overwhelming for a child and can make him feel even more helpless in a situation already fraught with danger. If the pressure persists, it can cripple his emotional and social progress. Instead of gathering strength from his childhood experiences of loss, he will be seriously weakened by the demands made on him. Many children become angry at being robbed of their childhood, and they are saddened, sometimes beyond repair, by having so few of their own needs gratified.

For a lot of people, divorce is so devastating that even with an excellent support system, they benefit immensely from counseling. The loss involved in divorce is so drastic that generally full recovery takes at least a year. Frequently, three to five years following the divorce, a parent continues to experience pain, resentment, and anger. Counseling might help you move through the process more easily and quickly, and it can help you handle the painful losses of divorce in ways that will help you grow emotionally. When you get the help and support you need, you are far more likely to respond sensitively and appropriately to your child's needs. And if you want to provide your child with additional support, you might consider counseling for him, too.

The monumental challenge of helping children cope with divorce in a healthy way begins with the seemingly simple question of how to tell them. During this difficult transition, you might need to refresh your skills in using feeling talk to communicate sensitively and honestly with your child.

A case in point...

Suzie and I talked about how we would tell our four-and-a-half-year-old son that I was moving out of the house. We chose a time for the talk when we were well rested and our painful emotions were somewhat subdued. I carried David into the den, and we all sat down on the rug in front of the fireplace.

"Davie," I said, holding him close, "we have something important to tell you. Daddy and Mommy are not happy living together, so I'm going to live in another house. You'll live here with Mommy part of the time and with me at my house part of the time. I'll talk with you on the telephone when you're with Mommy, and Mommy will talk with you on the phone when you're with me. You can help me pack tomorrow and come with me to see where I'm going to live."

David clung to me and began to cry. Suzie and I cried, too.

"This is not your fault, Davie," I said. "It's Daddy and Mommy's problem. Remember we both love you very much."

"Don't go, Daddy. Please," David sobbed.

"I'm sorry," I said. "I know this makes you sad."

Suzie hugged and kissed him and said, "We're sad right now, but it will get better."

It was not an easy time for anyone in this family, but the care, honesty, and sensitivity that David's parents put into how, when, and where to tell him the sad news was as good a first step in a difficult process as they could have made.

Often it falls to the parent who stays in the family home to communicate with the child about what has happened. Although generally children are aware of changes in the emotional tone of the family, they most likely have no idea that conflict can lead to the loss of a parent. If that news comes out of the blue for the child, it will be particularly painful for him. A counselor or parenting class can provide support and information for a single parent who has to cope with this.

Being flexible about scheduling visits so that neither parent forfeits needed time with them also helps children cope with this major loss. Judith Wallerstein encourages parents to work together on schedules so the child feels comfortable with new routines. This builds flexibility in youngsters, particularly when scheduled visits aren't cancelled. If for some reason the visit must be rescheduled, you need to give your child as much notice and explanation as possible.[22]

Fighting over the children, saying abusive things about each other, and blaming the other parent in front of them is harmful to children. Long after a husband and wife are divorced, they will still be their children's parents. Tugging at a child's loyalty adds to his stress, and in the long run it generally backfires on the parent who initiates it. The day will come when he will put his life story together in his own way, and he may well grow up to resent a parent who struggled to break his bond with his other parent.

A case in point...

My in-laws divorced when my wife, Heather, was an infant. While Heather was growing up, her mother never ceased to bad-mouth her father, and Heather had no relationship with him. I'll never forget her sad look and downcast eyes every time her mother visited and began to say unkind things about her father. There's no question that a father or mother who berates a former spouse causes a child tremendous emotional pain. I made up my mind that if Heather and I ever split up, I would never do that.

POWER POINTS

- ✓ Help your child understand the difference between feeling sad and feeling responsible.
- ✓ Use your support system.
- ✓ Consider counseling if hostility is present.
- ✓ Remember that though you are no longer married, you will always be parents.

When parents who divorce manage to dissolve their marital relationship without hostility, they are more likely to retain positive relationships with their children. Studies on children of divorce have shown that they do better in their social, academic, and emotional lives one year after the divorce if the parents have exposed them to minimal hostility and conflict. Feeling talk can buffer children from most of the negative consequences of divorce except for sad feelings. Parents who actively coach their children emotionally through the divorce process can markedly reduce the health, behavioral, and interpersonal problems that children of divorce often experience. There is no age at which divorce doesn't have the potential to be extremely hurtful to a child, but as Penelope Leach has written:

> Nobody would bring a child into the world intending to face him with such disruption but, if you do not have the power to prevent it, you do have the power to see him through it, so don't waste unnecessary energy on feeling that you have failed him forever. You have not failed him by separating; you will only have done so if, between you, he loses out on love.[23]

> *When we hold onto the past and wrap ourselves in the security of yesterday, we may miss the great blessing God has for us today.*
>
> WILLIAM L. COLEMAN

Disasters

Whether it's a fire, a flood, or an act of war, a disaster strikes unexpectedly and with such force that it can require all your attention and energy to cope with it. Even for those fortunate enough not to suffer the death of loved ones, catastrophes can result in the loss of home and most or all family possessions, including a lifetime of mementos. Nevertheless, parents can use a major catastrophe, just as they can any loss, as an opportunity to help their child develop emotional resiliency.

Depending on the age of the child, sensitive responding ranges from merely resuming the status quo as quickly as possible to extensive verbal and physical soothing and reassurance. Above all, take care of yourself first. When the painful and frightening aspects of a disaster impact your infant, the key is for you to remain calm, because if you don't, you won't be able to soothe your child.

A case in point...

In our sleepy little town of Coalinga, California, the ground began to tremble and buildings moved. Everything seemed to be crashing and falling. Beds rocked and rolled. Water sloshed out of swimming pools, and electric wires swung and swayed. There was a noise like a freight train passing through. It was noisy and frightening for everybody.

My eleven-month-old daughter awakened in her crib and began to scream. I stumbled to the crib and gathered her to my breast. But she just screamed more loudly when she felt my trembling body.

Even a very young child reads his caretakers' emotions quite accurately and can sense fear in them. When disaster hits, the key is to stay calm. Raised voices and yelling increase panic. It takes experience and practice to suppress feelings of panic and remain calm during an emergency.

A case in point...

During the French and Arab War of the 1950s, I lived in Africa with my six-month-old daughter, Kay. One afternoon my friend, Alice, and her six-month-old daughter, Sue, were visiting us. During teatime, fighting broke out in nearby Medina. Alice grabbed Sue and clutched her to her breast. Feeling her mother's fright, Sue started to scream and in her terror clutched Alice's double strand of pearls and sent them flying across the room.

I picked up Kay from her bassinet, pillow and all, and placed her in the bathtub to protect her from stray bullets. She couldn't feel how frightened I was because the pillow kept her from feeling my tense body and pounding heart.

Your toddler may be more aware of and responsive to major environmental disasters than an infant would be, but he will still take his cues almost exclusively from those around him, particularly his primary caregivers. He will react to the loud sounds and visible destruction of his environment by crying and signaling his fear and insecurity. Just as your response to a terrifying incident could be fight or flight, a terrorized baby may act out in tantrums and aggressive behaviors, or he may become extra clingy and afraid to have you out of his sight. However he expresses it, he is communicating his need for attention and soothing.

Because they have become attached both to people other than parents and to material belongings, preschoolers will grieve when a natural disaster results in loss of home and possessions and separation from people. When a preschooler finds his room, toys, books, and everything in his world utterly destroyed, he feels sad and lost. Feeling talk is an excellent way to help him get through such an experience. Naming his feelings of loss, sadness, and fear is the first step. Validating his feelings and offering verbal and physical soothing and support are next. Active problem solving and exploring ways to begin again follow quite naturally when feelings have been adequately expressed, named, accepted, and validated.

Like people of all ages, when young children are extremely frightened, they might "freeze" in terror. This is not the time for raised voices, threats, or demands that can only increase their fear. Remain as calm as possible while you protect yourself and your child by whatever measures are appropriate.

If you move to an area that has a disaster potential you aren't familiar with, learn what you can about likely events so that if one occurs, you won't be taken completely by surprise and will be able to focus on what needs to be done.

A case in point...

Our one-and-a-half-year-old son, Harold, was just drifting off to sleep when the sun set on a typical summer evening on our Midwest farm. Three hours later he woke up when my husband began shouting for everyone to get up and to the basement for safety. The howling wind and slamming doors were painfully loud, and Harold began to scream. The piercing sound of shattering glass scared him even more.

I picked him up, hurried to the basement, and laid him in the bed we kept set up for him there. While the wind roared and the rain pelted the ground above the basement, I stroked him gently and sang to him. Soon he fell back to sleep.

For after all, the best thing one can do when it is raining, is to let it rain.

HENRY WADSWORTH LONGFELLOW

Although Harold's parents had felt understandably frightened, they had survived other tornadoes and knew what to do. They managed to act calmly enough that Harold was unaware of the destruction going on all around him. Perhaps because of this and several subsequent protected experiences with tornadoes, Harold continues to live in the same tornado belt without undue fear.

Today, images of disasters around the world are televised almost continuously. It's important to remember that your child's age largely determines the amount of information he will be able to handle. If a disaster occurs that is widely reported, you should carefully monitor his access to television. Viewing the pictures over and over could increase his anxiety.

A preschooler will feel the losses of a catastrophic event more keenly than toddlers or infants, but, as with any loss, his more developed communication skills give you another way to comfort him. Art therapy is one way to help an older child structure his emotional experiences as he copes with loss.

A case in point...

When my cousin, William was four, he was living with our grandmother. One day while they were coming home from the store, they saw huge flames spiraling into the sky. By the time they got home, firemen were spraying water on the roof in a futile attempt to extinguish the flames shooting out of the roof.

The house was completely destroyed, and Gran and William moved into another house. Gran later told me that when she tried to get William to talk about his feelings, he withdrew, so she called the family doctor, who referred them to a grief counselor.

William drew the red flames and burned structures of the house and talked with the counselor. Finally he got so he could talk with Gran about the fire, too.

As awful as it was, William's experience turned out to be an invaluable opportunity for him to learn good grieving. His grandmother, who had been both mother and father to him, died right after he graduated from high school, and he was devastated. At first he didn't know where to turn, but finally he called Mr. Fingherstine. William had grown close to Mr. Fingherstine during his four years of high school and saw him as something of a father figure. When William told him of his loss, Mr. Fingherstine invited him over and encouraged him to talk about what had happened.

Though the death of his grandmother was the worst loss William had ever experienced, he wasn't trapped in stuffed, crippling grief. He had learned the skills of good grieving by coping with smaller losses, and he was able to reach out to others for help, move forward, and eventually find the gift hidden in the loss.

Many people come into our lives and quickly go, but some stay for a while and give us a deeper understanding of what is truly important in life. They touch our souls, and we gain strength from the footprints they have left on our hearts. William's grandmother was one of those people, and he realized how blessed he had been to have had her with him, loving and supporting him for so long.

Power Points

- ✓ Take care of yourself.
- ✓ Remain as calm as possible.
- ✓ Monitor access to images on television.
- ✓ Use feeling talk to process the event once it's over.

As the gifts of the wise ones were…we are not told whose gift was gold or whose was the gift of myrrh.

Edmund Vance Cooke

Epilogue

Reaping the Rewards of a Resilient Child

Grief should be
Like joy, majestic, cleansing, raising, making free;
Strong to consume small troubles, to commend
Great thoughts, grave thoughts,
thoughts lasting to the end.

Aubrey Thomas de Vere

We live in a society that places great value on winning. Losing is for…well, losers. Just recently, this comment appeared on the Internet: "We often hear about teaching children to be 'good losers.' Why on earth would we want any child to learn to be good at losing?" I hope that this book has helped answer that question. Losing is the price we pay for living. The bad news is that with every loss comes pain and grief. The good news is that gifts are hidden in all the losses of childhood.

Parents have always wanted to protect their children from pain and loss, but not until recently have we begun to understand how important it is to prepare children as well as protect them. Grief that is denied or not fully experienced can emotionally cripple a human being for years, even for life. As parents, when you learn and then teach your children good grieving, you give them the gift of a lifetime, for grieving is the process that unwraps the gift of loss. It is a process that must be taught, and as a parent, you are your child's best teacher.

> *One father is more than a hundred schoolmasters.*
>
> SEVENTEENTH-CENTURY ENGLISH PROVERB

I remember when leukemia was slowly weakening Aunt Mattie, how my father carefully prepared us for her death. At the end of each day, all ten of us would wait patiently on the front porch for Dad to come back from visiting Aunt Mattie. Every evening when he arrived home, he would get out of the car and walk toward us as we ran to meet him. Giving us a hug, he would say, "Aunt Mattie is very sick."

Each day the report was worse. Then one day when Dad came home, he didn't get out of the car as usual. Somehow we knew. At last he got out of the car and walked slowly toward us. Wrapping us in his arms, he said, "Aunt Mattie died."

Aunt Mattie's coffin lay in her living room surrounded with flowers. Dad described how she looked with her head on a white satin pillow in a beautiful white and gold coffin. He said, "Her hands feel cold, but you can touch her if you'd like." We didn't have to go if we didn't want to, but we wanted to. With his arms around us, Dad took us two at a time to view Aunt Mattie. I touched her white hair, felt the beautiful white satin pillow, and breathed in the aroma of all the beautiful flowers. I cherished that good-bye.

Dad was a good teacher.

It takes time, empathy, and honesty to teach your children good grieving. But when you are willing to cultivate in yourself the traits you wish to see in them, you can forge a relationship with them that is based on mutual trust and respect. As a result, you reap many times over the rewards of having raised what Robert Browning called "a happy-tempered bringer of the best out of the worst."

For a child who experiences good grieving, losses from small to profound can result not only in a lifelong emotional resiliency, but also in character traits like self-discipline, honesty, trust, compassion, responsibility, authenticity, courage, selflessness, gratitude, and a capacity for intimacy. In time, such children are likely to become their parents' best friends. Some day someone may look at your relationship with your children and exclaim, "Aren't you lucky!"

Luck, however, usually happens because somewhere along the line preparation met opportunity. When you learn good grieving yourself and then identify opportunities to coach your children through the losses of early childhood, you turn those losses into a gift that keeps on giving.

Every good and perfect gift is from above, coming down from the Father of the heavenly lights.

JAMES 1:17

STRUGGLE

Beth Landers

A man found a cocoon of the emperor moth and took it home to watch it emerge. One day a small opening appeared, and for several hours the moth struggled but couldn't seem to force its body past a certain point. Deciding something was wrong, the man took scissors and snipped the remaining bit of cocoon. The moth emerged easily, its body large and swollen, the wings small and shriveled.

He expected that in a few hours the wings would spread out in their natural beauty, but they did not. Instead of developing into a creature free to fly, the moth spent its life dragging around a swollen body and shriveled wings.

The constricting cocoon and the struggle necessary to pass through the tiny opening are God's way of forcing fluid from the body into the wings. The "merciful" snip was, in reality, cruel. Sometimes the struggle is exactly what we need.

About the Author

Grace E. Davis has spent over two decades in intensive study and clinical research in the fields of childhood trauma, child development, and the human grieving process.

Grace graduated *cum laude* from California State University, Fresno (CSUF), with a bachelor's degree in nursing, is accredited as a public health nurse/registered nurse, holds a California health and development credential, and has taken advanced classes in early childhood education. She completed an independent study on childhood trauma and children's hospice in London and Oxford, England, and she attended the Tenth International Conference on "Children in Turmoil" in Dublin, Ireland in 1982.

Grace's thirty-nine-year nursing career included fourteen years as a school nurse in Fresno County special education schools for the severely disabled. She developed and conducted in-service classes on childhood loss for teachers, parents, and children and taught a unit on children in trauma at CSUF. She spent eight years in the field of hospice care and helped develop a hospice program under the guidance of Sister Raphael, director of the St. Agnes Hospice of Fresno. Her first book, *Helping Your Young Child Face the Reality of Death,* was published in 1986.

Grace was born on a farm near Redfield, South Dakota, the seventh of thirteen children. She now lives in Fresno with her husband. She has two children and four grandchildren.

Judith St. Pierre, PhD, is a former professor and professional editor who now does freelance writing and editing from her home in Central Oregon. She is editorial director of Abiding Books and can be reached at www.abidingbooks.com.

Notes

1. For ease of reading, throughout the book I use male pronouns (he, him, his) to refer to both boys and girls.
2. John M. Gottman, *Raising an Emotionally Intelligent Child* (Simon & Schuster, 1998).
3. Harry Emerson Fosdick, *Twelve Tests of Character* (Harper & Brothers Publishers, 1923).
4. Alan D. Wolfelt, *Healing Your Grieving Heart for Kids* (Companion Press, 2001).
5. Evelyn Thoman and Sue Browder, *Born Dancing: How Intuitive Parents Understand Their Baby's Unspoken Language and Natural Rhythm* (HarperCollins, 1987), 27, 38.
6. Frederick Leboyer, *Loving Hands* (Alfred A. Knopf, 1976).
7. Bruno Bettleheim, "The Importance of Play," *Atlantic Monthly* (March 1987): 35–46.
8. Frederick Leboyer, *Childbirth without Violence* (Alfred A. Knopf, 1975), 15.
9. Christine Benvenuto, *Mothering Magazine* (November/December 1999): 38.
10. Daniel Hughes, *Facilitating Developmental Attachment* (Jason Aronson, 1997), 204.
11. "Between the Lines," *The Doula* (Fall 1993): 2.
12. T. Barry Brazelton, *Touchpoints: Your Child's Emotional and Behavioral Development, Birth–3: The Essential Reference for the Early Years* (Perseus Press, 1992), 170.
13. Penelope Leach, *Your Baby and Child from Birth to Age Five* (Alfred A. Knopf, 1989), 315.
14. This chapter is based on the stages of grieving described in Dr. Elisabeth Kübler-Ross's pathbreaking book, *On Death and Dying,* which explores denial, isolation, anger, bargaining, depression, and acceptance as the emotional reactions to death.
15. C. Wayne Standiford, *Bury Me with Soldiers: One Grunt's Honest Story About Vietnam* (1st Books, 2003), 35–6.
16. Ibid., 36.
17. Ibid.
18. Ibid., 61.
19. Jennifer Rothschild, *Lessons I Learned in the Dark: Steps to Walking by Faith, Not by Sight* (Multnomah, 2002), 182.
20. Laurel Seiler Brunvoll and David G. Seiler, *Life on Hold: Finding Hope in the Face of Serious Illness* (Multnomah, 2001), 162–3.
21. Standiford, *Bury Me with Soldiers*, 146.
22. Judith Wallerstein and Joan Berlin Kelly, *Surviving the Breakup: How Children and Parents Cope with Divorce* (Basic Books, 1996).
23. Leach, *Your Baby and Child from Birth to Age Five*, 273.

Bibliography

Books Parents Can Read to Children

There is no warmer feeling for a parent and a child than rocking to the rhythm of a story. The child feels a sense of belonging as he listens to the comforting sound of your voice, and he quickly learns to seek this pleasure. As he grows, books can help him learn to cope with life's ups and downs. They can help him understand his hidden fears and give him insights into solving problems.

Here is a list of books that will help you lay a strong foundation of emotional communication with your child. There are many more waiting for your child in libraries and bookstores. When you read to your child, keep these things in mind:

- Be sure to read the book before you read it to your child.
- Read with expression and for only as long as you're holding your child's attention.
- After the story, listen to the child's response before you talk about it.
- The book's age category is not as important as the child's interest in and readiness for the subject.

Feelings

Alexander, Martha. *I'll Protect You from the Jungle Beasts.* Dial Books for Young Readers, 1983.
Toddlers and preschoolers
Shows the need for a support system.

Aliki. *Feelings.* HarperTrophy, 1986.
Preschoolers
Helps children deal with anger, fear, jealously, guilt, and loneliness.

Arnold, Katya. *That Apple Is Mine!* Holiday House, 2000.
Toddlers and preschoolers
Rabbit, crow, and hedgehog fight over an apple until bear persuades them to share.

Balian, Lorna. *The Aminal.* Humbug Books, 1994.
Toddlers and preschoolers
A boy's friends imagine a large, fearful monster before they see what he really found.

Bang, Molly Garrett. *When Sophie Gets Angry—Really, Really Angry.* Scholastic, 1999.
Preschoolers
When Sophie gets angry with her sister, she climbs a big beech tree to calm down.

Bartholomew, Bartholomew. *Jimmy and the White Lie.* Concordia, 1976.
Preschool
Jimmy learns the importance of telling the truth.

Bateman, Teresa. *Farm Flu.* Albert Whitman & Co., 2001.
Toddlers and preschoolers
When the farm animals seem to catch the flu, a boy does his best to take care of them.

Bogacki, Tomek. *I Hate You! I Like You!* Farrar Straus & Giroux, 1997.
Preschoolers
A small creature dislikes everything about a large creature who wants to be friends.

Burningham, John. *The Friend.* Candlewick Press, 1996.
Preschoolers
Two friends play together well, although sometimes they argue.

Bibliography

Clark, Emma Chichester. *Where Are You, Blue Kangaroo?* Doubleday, 2001.
Toddlers and preschoolers
Lili learns about friendship and responsibility.

Cosby, Bill. *My Big Lie.* Cartwheel Books, 1999.
Little Bill tells a big fib about why he is late getting home for dinner.

Couture, Susan Arkin. *Melanie Jane.* Harpercollins Juvenile Books, 1996.
Toddlers and preschoolers
When her mother won't change the color of the sky, Melanie Jane flies into a rage.

Day, Linda Johnson. *The Mouse and the Rock.* Cal Valley Printing, 2000.
Preschoolers
Mouse overcomes obstacles and makes sacrifices to meet his goals.

Edens, Cooper. *If You're Afraid of the Dark, Remember the Night Rainbow.* Aladdin Library, 1991.
All ages
Proves that it's possible to face obstacles with a positive attitude.

Emberley, Ed. *Go Away, Big Green Monster!* Little Brown & Co., 1993.
Toddlers and preschoolers
Die-cut pages revealing bits of a monster help a child control nighttime fears.

Evans, Richard Paul. *The Dance.* Simon & Schuster Children's Publishing, 1999.
Preschoolers
A father watches his daughter dance through the various stages of her life.

Everitt, Betsy. *Mean Soup.* Voyager Books, 1995.
Toddlers and preschoolers
Horace feels mean at the end of a bad day until he helps his mother make mean soup.

Field, Rachel. *Prayer for a Child.* Little Simon, 1997.
Babies–preschoolers
Celebrates the love of friends and family and the universal protection of God.

Fowler, Allan. *Feeling Things.* Children's Press, 1991.
Toddlers and preschoolers
Discusses the sense of touch and how it tells us more about the world around us.

Fox, Mem. *Wilfrid Gordon McDonald Partridge.* Scott Foresman, 1989.
Toddlers and preschoolers
A boy tries to discover the meaning of memory so he can restore that of an elderly friend.

Fox, Mem, and Marla Frazee. *Harriet, You'll Drive Me Wild!* Voyager Books, 2003.
Preschoolers
When Harriet has a series of mishaps, her mother tries not to lose her temper.

Freymann, Saxton. *How Are You Peeling?* Arthur A. Levine, 1999.
Toddlers and preschoolers
Cute book about the moods of foods.

Gray, Kes, and Mary McQuillan. *The Get Well Soon Book: Good Wishes for Bad Times.* Millbrook, 2000.
Toddlers and preschoolers
Humorous examples help children empathize with others worse off than they.

Heide, Florence Parry. *Some Things Are Scary.* Candlewick Press, 2000.
Preschoolers
Scary things include moving and having a best friend whose best friend isn't you.

Helmer, Diana Star. *Let's Talk about Feeling Sad.* Powerkids Press, 2003.
Preschoolers
Talks about what makes people feel sad and how to handle their feelings.

Ho, Minfong. *Hush! A Thai Lullaby.* Orchard Books, 2000.
Babies–preschoolers
A mother tries to soothe her baby to sleep.

Hoban, Russell. *Bedtime for Frances.* HarperTrophy, 1995.
Toddlers and preschoolers
Opens up discussions of common fears and problems children have after dark.

Joosse, Barbara M. *Better with Two.* Harpercollins Juvenile Books, 1988.
Toddlers and preschoolers
Laura tries to make Mrs. Brady feel better when her dog dies.

________. *Dinah's Mad, Bad Wishes.* Harpercollins Juvenile Books, 1989.
Toddlers and preschoolers
Dinah wishes horrible things for her mother when the two have a quarrel.

________. *Mama, Do You Love Me?* Chronicle Books, 1998.
Babies–preschoolers
An Inuit girl uses her imagination to test her mother's love.

Joyce, William. *The Leaf Men and the Brave Good Bugs.* Laura Geringer, 1996.
Preschoolers
A magic, epic adventure and a salute to the power of memory, loyalty, and love.

Kraus, Robert. *Leo the Late Bloomer.* Harpercollins Juvenile Books, 1994.
Toddlers and preschoolers
A tiger cub eventually catches up to his more accomplished animal friends.

Kunhardt, Dorothy. *Pat the Bunny.* Golden Books, 2001.
Babies–toddlers.
Contains things to touch, move, and smell and hidden surprises to peek at.

Lucado, Max. *Just the Way You Are.* Crossway, 1999.
Preschoolers
In a family adopted by a king, the one willing to spend time with him wins his approval.

________. *You Are Special.* Crossway, 1997.
Toddlers and preschoolers
Punchinello's opinion of himself changes after talking to his Creator.

________. *Just in Case You Ever Wonder.* Thomas Nelson, 1992.
Toddlers and preschoolers
A parent tells a child how special she is, both to the parent and to God.

McBratney, Sam. *Guess How Much I Love You.* Candlewick Press, 1996.
All ages
Two bunnies' love for each other and a special love between a parent and a child.

Mayer, Mercer. *There's a Nightmare in My Closet.* Puffin, 1992.
Toddlers and preschoolers
At bedtime a boy confronts the nightmare in his closet.

Mundy, Michaelene. *Sad Isn't Bad.* Abbey Press, 1998.
Preschoolers
A good grieving guidebook for kids dealing with loss.

Modesitt, Jeanne. *Sometimes I Feel Like a Mouse.* Scholastic, 1992.
Babies–preschoolers
A delightful book about feelings.

Munsch, Robert. *I'll Love You Forever.* Firefly Books, 1988.
Preschoolers
As a child grows into an adult, he learns that love is forever.

Murphy, Mary. *I Feel Happy and Sad and Angry and Glad.* DK Ink, 2000.
Babies–preschoolers
Humorous way to teach children that feelings are okay and to help them use feeling talk.

Offerman, Lynn. *Little Teddy Bear's Happy Face, Sad Face.* Millbrook, 1999.
Babies–preschoolers
Teaches about different emotions while helping develop fine motor skills.

Parr, Todd. *The Feeling Book.* Megan Tingley, 2000.
Preschoolers
Encourages children to identify and label their constantly shifting emotions.

________. *Things That Make You Feel Good/Things That Make You Feel Bad.* Megan Tingley, 1999.
Babies–preschoolers
Sends a self-esteem message that children can grasp.

Politi, Leo. *Lito and the Clown.* Scribner, 1964.
Preschoolers
Lito deals with his sad and happy feelings when he loses his kitty and then finds him again.

________. *The Nicest Gift.* Atheneum, 1973.

Preschoolers
A little boy deals with feelings of loss and gain when he loses his dog and finds him again.

Rogers, Fred. *Making Friends.* Puffin, 1996.
Preschoolers
Describes the pleasures of friendship as well as potential problems and helpful solutions.

Schuette, Sarah L. *I Am Honest.* Pebble Books, 2002.
Toddlers and preschoolers
Simple text and photographs show the various ways children can be honest.

Sendak, Maurice. *Where the Wild Things Are.* HarperCollins, 1988.
Preschoolers
A boy sent to his room for being naughty wants to run away and join the "wild things."

Spelman, Cornelia Maud. *When I Care about Others.* Albert Whitman & Co., 2002.
Toddlers and preschoolers
A little bear helps youngsters understand the importance of the Golden Rule.

________. *When I Feel Angry.* Albert Whitman & Co., 2000.
Toddlers and preschoolers
A young rabbit talks about what makes her angry and how she can deal with her emotions.

Seuss, Dr. *Horton Hears a Who!* Random House, 1954.
Preschoolers
A person is a person, no matter how small, and should be cared for with love.

________. *My Many Colored Days.* Alfred A. Knopf, 1998.
Toddlers and preschoolers
Encourages talking about emotions and initiating discussions about anger management.

Tabor, Nancy Maria Grande. *We Are a Rainbow.* Charlesbridge Publishing, 1995.
Preschoolers
Builds bridges of understanding through simple comparisons of cultures.

Vail, Rachel. *Sometimes I'm Bombaloo.* Scholastic, 2000.
Toddlers and preschoolers
All kids get angry sometimes, but a tantrum isn't the way to cope.

Van Leeuwen, Jean. *"Wait for Me!" Said Maggie McGee.* Phyllis Fogelman Books, 2001.
Toddlers and preschoolers
Maggie eventually outgrows the disadvantages of being the youngest in the family.

Viorst Judith. *Alexander and the Terrible, Horrible, No Good, Very Bad Day.* Aladdin, 1987.
Toddlers and preschoolers
Alexander gets in touch with his feelings on a bummer day.

Wild, Margaret. *The Pocket Dogs.* Scholastic, 2001.
Toddlers and preschoolers
Mr. Pocket and Buff experience strong emotions when Biff falls out of Mr. Pocket's pocket.

Wilhelm, Hans. *Tyrone the Double Dirty Rotten Cheater.* Scholastic, 1991.
Preschoolers
A sneaky dinosaur who wins by cheating gets his just deserts.

Ziefert, Harriet. *Clara Ann Cookie, Go to Bed!* Houghton Mifflin, 2000.
Preschoolers
Clara resists going to go to bed, so her teddy bear does, too.

Zolotow, Charlotte. *The Hating Book.* HarperTrophy, 1989.
Preschoolers
Shows that friends can fight and then forgive and make up.

________. *One Step Two.* William Morrow, 1981.
Babies–preschoolers
Mothers show their love by giving their children all the love they need.

Separation

Brown, Margaret Wise. *Goodnight Moon.* HarperFestival, 1991.
Babies–preschoolers
Bunny lovingly says "good-night" to everything.

________. *The Runaway Bunny.* HarperFestival, 1991.
Toddlers and preschoolers
Bunny's imaginary game of hide-and-seek and the mother who finds him every time.

Bunting, Eve. *Terrible Things.* Jewish Publication Society, 1996.
Preschoolers
Encourages children to stand up for what they think is right.

Corey, Dorothy. *You Go Away.* Albert Whitman & Co., 1999.
Babies and toddlers
Describes a child's everyday separations and reunions with parents or caretakers.

Bibliography

Crary, Elizabeth. *I'm Lost.* Parenting Press, 1996.
Preschoolers
Lost, Gabriela solves her problem.

________. *Mommy, Don't Go.* Parenting Press, 1996.
Toddlers and preschoolers
Mother helps her child when she leaves by telling her when she will return.

Fowler, Susi Gregg, and Jim Fowler. *I'll See You When the Moon Is Full.* Greenwillow, 1994.
Toddlers and preschoolers
Gabe's father explains that he will be back from a business trip when the moon is full.

Garland, Sarah. *All Gone.* Puffin, 1991.
Babies
Emphasizes the concept of "all gone."

Goennel, Heidi. *Sometimes I Like to Be Alone.* Little, Brown & Co., 1989.
Toddlers and preschoolers
Text describes and illustrations depict some of the special things that you can do alone.

Johnson, Paul Brett. *Lost.* Orchard Books, 1996.
Preschoolers
A young girl never gives up hope that her lost beagle will be found.

Kirk, David. *Little Miss Spider.* Scholastic, 2003.
Babies and toddlers
On her first day of life, little spider searches for her mother.

McCloskey, Robert. *Blueberries for Sal.* Puffin, 1976.
Preschoolers
Sal and her mother search for blueberries at the same time a mother and her cub do.

Merriam, Eve. *Daddies at Work.* Little Simon, 1991.
Toddlers and preschoolers
Talks about separation when Daddy goes to work.

________. *Mommies at Work.* Random House, 1968.
Toddlers and preschoolers
No matter what kind of job Mommy has, her favorite thing is coming home to you.

Nethery, Mary. *Hannah and Jack.* Atheneum, 1996.
Toddlers and preschoolers
Hannah goes to her grandma's and has to leave her cat, Jack, at home.

Rogers, Fred. *Going to the Hospital.* Puffin, 1997.
Toddlers and preschoolers
Describes what can happen during a stay in the hospital.

Tyler, Linda Wagner. *When Daddy Comes Home.* Viking, 1988.
Toddlers and preschoolers
A young hippo stays up until his father comes home so they can spend time together.

Viorst, Judith. *Good-Bye Book.* Aladdin, 1992.
Toddlers and preschoolers
A child complains when his parents go out and leave him with a babysitter.

Waber, Bernard. *Ira Sleeps Over.* Houghton Mifflin/Walter Lorraine Books, 1987.
Preschoolers
Helps prepare a child for overnight visits and peer pressure.

Waddell, Martin. *Owl Babies.* Candlewick Press, 1996.
Babies–preschoolers
Three baby owls awake to find their mother gone.

Zion, Gene. *Harry the Dirty Dog.* HarperTrophy, 1976.
Preschoolers
Harry tries to escape a bath by running away.

Starting Preschool

Berenstain, Stan, and Jan Berenstain. *The Berenstain Bears Go to School.* Random House, 1978.
Preschoolers
Sister Bear conquers her fear of first day of kindergarten.

Cuddy, Robbin. *Pooh's First Day of School.* Disney Press, 1999.
Toddlers and preschoolers
Pooh embodies the innocence of a preschooler while offering comfort and reassuring silliness.

Conlin, Susan. *All My Feelings at Preschool: Nathan's Day.* Parenting Press, 1991.
Preschoolers
A day at preschool inspires a range of feelings from confident to rejected, happy to angry.

McQuade, Jacqueline. *At Nursery School with Teddy Bear.* Chrysalis Books, 2001.
Babies–preschoolers
Teddy is ready to meet new friends and learn new things.

Ovenell-Carter, Julie. *Adam's Daycare.* Firefly Books, 1997.
Babies–preschoolers
Adam's experiences at a family-run day care.

Penn, Audrey. *The Kissing Hand.* Child Welfare League of America, 1993.
Toddlers and preschoolers
Chester the raccoon is reluctant to go to kindergarten for the first time.

Worth, Bonnie. *I Can Go to Pre-School.* Golden Books, 1997.
Babies–preschoolers
Kermit says he's big enough now to stay away from home each day to go to preschool.

Weaning

Deutschbein, Mary Joan. *Maggie's Weaning.* La Leche League, 1999.
Toddlers and preschoolers
Deals with the bittersweet experience of weaning.

Gikow, Louise. *Bye-Bye, Pacifier.* Golden Books, 1992.
Preschoolers
Piggy says good-bye to her pacifier.

Graham, Bob. *The Red Woolen Blanket.* Candlewick Press, 2001.
Preschoolers
Little Julia carries her blanket everywhere, until one day she outgrows it.

Henkes, Kevin. *Owen.* Greenwillow, 1993.
Toddlers and preschoolers
Owens's parents try to get him to give up his favorite blanket before he starts school.

Lindgren, Barbro, and Olof Landstriom. *Benny and the Binky.* R & S Books, 2002.
Toddlers and preschoolers
Benny wants to share his baby brother's pacifier.

Weiss, Ellen. *Bye-Bye, Bottle.* Golden Books, 1991.
Toddlers and preschoolers
Kermit realizes that he has to say good-bye to the bottle before he starts using the cup.

Toilet Training

Cole, Joanna. *Your New Potty.* William Morrow, 1989.
Toddlers and preschoolers
Teaches small children how and when to use the potty.

Falwell, Cathryn. *P.J. and Puppy.* Clarion Books, 1997.
Toddlers and preschoolers
P.J. uses a new potty, and his new puppy uses papers.

Frankel, Alona. *Once Upon a Potty—Boy.* HarperFestival, 1999.
Toddlers and preschoolers
A book to buy along with a boy's new potty.

________. *Once Upon a Potty—Girl.* HarperFestival, 1999.
Toddlers and preschoolers
A book to buy along with a girl's new potty.

Rogers, Fred. *Going to the Potty.* Puffin, 1997.
Toddlers and preschoolers
Talks about growing up and using new skills.

Wilson-Max, Ken. *Flush the Potty!* Cartwheel, 2000.
Toddlers and preschoolers
Encourages young children to say bye-bye to diapers.

Worth, Bonnie. *I Can Go Potty.* Golden Books, 1999.
Toddlers and preschoolers
Relates the steps of using the potty, from going to wiping to washing hands.

Sibling Birth

Aliki. *Welcome, Little Baby.* Greenwillow, 1987.
Toddlers and preschoolers
A mother welcomes her newborn and tells her how she will grow.

Alexander, Martha G. *Nobody Asked Me if I Wanted a Baby Sister.* Demco Media, 1977.
Toddlers and preschoolers
Big brother tries to give away his baby sister.

Anholt, Catherine. *Aren't You Lucky!* Joy, 1991.
Toddlers and preschoolers
A warm story about when a baby is added to the family.

Ashbe, Jeanne. *What's Inside.* Kane/Miller Book Publishers, 2000.
Toddlers and preschoolers
Helps toddlers understand what's happening inside Mommy's tummy.

Baronian, Jean Baptiste. *Will You Still Love Me?* Chronicle Books, 2001.
Preschoolers
Polo faces the birth of a sibling.

Berenstain, Stan. *The Birds, the Bees, and the Berenstain Bears.* Random House, 2000.
Toddlers and preschoolers
Sister Bear wants to know where the baby comes from and how it's going to get out of Mama's body.

Brown, Marc. *Arthur's Baby.* Little Brown & Co., 1998.
Toddlers and preschoolers
At first Arthur isn't sure about the new baby.

Clifton, Lucille. *Everett Anderson's Nine Month Long.* Henry Holt, 1978.
Preschoolers
A family welcomes a new baby to share their love.

Cole, Joanne. *The New Baby at Your House.* HarperTrophy, 1999.
Toddlers and preschoolers
Prepares children for the ups and downs of having a new baby in the house.

________. *I'm a Big Brother.* William Morrow, 1997.
Toddlers and preschoolers
A young boy welcomes home his new baby brother.

________. *I'm a Big Sister*. William Morrow, 1997.
Toddlers and preschoolers
A young girl welcomes home her new baby sister.

Coville, Bruce. *The Lapsnatcher.* Troll Association, 1997.
Toddlers and preschoolers
Helps children deal with a new baby in the house.

Cowell, Cressida. *What Shall We Do with the Boo-Hoo Baby?* Scholastic, 2003.
Toddlers and preschoolers
A baby's animal friends try to figure out what will calm him down.

DePaola, Tomie. *A New Barker in the House.* Putnam, 2002.
Toddlers and preschoolers
Twins are excited when they hear their family is adopting a Hispanic boy.

Farmer, Patti. *What's He Doing Now?* Firefly Books, 1998.
Preschoolers
Captures the curiosity of a child who is awaiting the birth of a sibling.

Hiatt, Fred. *Baby Talk.* Margaret K. McElderry, 1999.
Preschoolers
Joey connects with his new baby brother by speaking in their own special language.

Hoban, Russell. *A Baby Sister for Frances.* HarperTrophy, 1976.
Toddlers and preschoolers
Makes any brother or sister feel better about a new sibling

Keats, Ezra Jack. *Peter's Chair.* Puffin, 1998.
Babies–preschoolers
Peter runs away when his old furniture is painted for his new baby sister.

L'Engle, Madeleine. *The Other Dog.* SeaStar Books, 2001.
Preschoolers
A precocious poodle is upstaged by a baby.

Limbacher, Phyllis Tildes. *Billy's Big-Boy Bed.* Charlesbridge, 2003.
Toddlers and preschoolers
Billy isn't sure he's ready for a big-boy bed.

Palatini, Margie. *Good As Goldie.* Disney Press, 2000.
Toddlers and preschoolers
A big sister lists all the things she can do that her baby brother cannot.

Rogers, Fred. *Let's Talk about It: Adoption.* Puffin, 1998.
Toddlers and preschoolers
Discusses some of the changes a new baby can cause in the lives of older siblings.

Scott, Ann Herbert. *On Mother's Lap.* Clarion Books, 1992.
Toddlers and preschoolers
An Intuit boy discovers there is room for him and his baby sister on their mother's lap.

Mario, Heidi Stetson. *I'd Rather Have an Iguana.* Charlesbridge, 1998.
Toddlers and preschoolers
A young girl resents her new baby brother at first.

Winter, Susan. *A Baby Just Like Me.* DK Publishing, 1994.
Toddlers and preschoolers.
Martha is disappointed with her new baby sister.

Wishinsky, Frieda. *Oonga Boonga.* Dutton Books, 1999.
Preschoolers
Big brother has just the right touch when it comes to getting the baby to stop crying.

Moving

Aliki. *Best Friends Together Again.* Greenwillow, 1995.
Preschoolers
Robert's friend moved away but comes back to visit.

Bibliography

Asch, Frank. *Goodbye, House.* Scott Foresman, 1989.
Toddlers and preschoolers
A family says good-bye to each room as the moving van waits.

Banks, Ann. *Goodbye, House: A Kid's Guide to Moving.* Knopf Books for Young Readers, 1999.
Preschoolers
A hands-on guide and activity book designed to help kids handle moving to a new home.

Berenstain, Jan, and Stan Berenstain. *The Berenstain Bears' Moving Day.* Random House, 1981.
Preschoolers
How Brother Bear feels when the Bear family moves to the tree house.

Carlstrom, Nancy White. *I'm Not Moving, Mama!* Aladdin Library, 1999.
Toddlers and preschoolers
A mother tells her child why she does not wish to leave him behind.

Couric, Katie. *The Brand New Kid.* Doubleday, 2000.
Preschoolers
Talks about the importance of tolerance, kindness, and compassion in our daily lives.

Friday, Beverly, and David Friday. *Time to Go.* Harcourt Young Classics, 1990.
Preschoolers
As he and his family prepare to leave, a child takes one last look at their farm.

Hoff, Syd. *Who Will Be My Friends?* HarperTrophy, 1985.
Preschoolers
Freddie likes his new house, but he needs new friends.

Johnson, Angela. *The Leaving Morning.* Orchard Books, 1992.
Preschoolers
Captures the bittersweet feelings that accompany moving day.

Johnston, Tony. *The Quilt Story.* Putnam Publishing Group, 1985.
Preschoolers
A pioneer mother stitches a quilt to warm and comfort her daughter during a move.

Komaiko, Leah. *Annie Bananie.* Yearling Books, 1998.
Preschoolers
An excellent book to ease the hurt moving causes a young child.

Rogers, Fred. *Moving.* Putnam Publishing Group, 1987.
Toddlers and preschoolers
Describes how children feel about moving and how to help them.

Smith, Miriam. *Annie and Moon: A Story.* Gareth Stevens, 1989.
Preschoolers
Her little black cat, Moon, gives Annie feelings of security during a series of moves.

Tobias, Tobi. *Moving Day*. Alfred A. Knopf, 1976.
Preschoolers
A stuffed toy bear helps comfort a little girl through the turmoil of moving day.

Viorst, Judith. *Alexander Who's Not (Do You Hear Me? I Mean It!) Going to Move.* Atheneum, 1995.
Preschoolers
Alexander is angry that his family has to move one thousand miles away.

Waber, Bernard. *Ira Says Goodbye.* Houghton Mifflin/Walter Lorraine Books, 1991.
Toddlers and preschoolers
Ira is surprised to discover that his best friend feels happy about having to move to a new town.

Wilhelm, Hans. *A New Home, A New Friend.* Random House, 1988.
Preschoolers
Michael's anxieties over moving to a new house are alleviated by the friendship of a large dog.

Zelonky, Joy. *My Best Friend Moved Away.* Chariot Family Publishers, 1986.
Preschoolers
When his best friend moves away, Brian tries to cope with his feelings of loss.

Zolotow, Charlotte. *Janey.* Harpercollins Juvenile Books, 1973.
Preschoolers
A young girl describes the loneliness she feels after her best friend moves away.

Death of a Pet

Brown, Margaret Wise. *The Dead Bird.* William Morrow, 2004.
Preschooler
Talks about the death and mourning for a pet bird.

Cohen, Miriam. *Jim's Dog Muffins.* Picture Yearling, 1996.
Preschoolers
A boy mourning the death of his dog needs a support group.

Johnson, Paul Brett, and Celeste Lewis. *Lost.* Orchard Books, 1996.
Preschoolers
Celeste's parents help her through the grieving process after she loses her dog.

Kirkpatrick, June. *Barn Kitty.* Gently Worded Books, 1999.
Preschoolers
A gentle approach to helping children cope with the death of a beloved pet.

Mills, Joyce C. *Gentle Willow.* Magination, 2003.
Preschoolers
A hope-filled metaphor for emphasizing transformation and the healing power of love.

Rogers, Fred. *When a Pet Dies.* Puffin, 1998.
Preschoolers
Explores the frustration, sadness, and loneliness youngsters feel when a pet dies.

Rylant, Cynthia. *Cat Heaven.* Scholastic, 1997.
Toddlers and preschoolers
If you have ever had a special cat in your life, you know there's a cat heaven.

Smith, Maggie. *Desser the Best Ever Cat.* Dragonfly, 2003.
Preschoolers
A heartwarming, cathartic book for anyone who has ever loved and lost a cat.

Sanford, Doris. *It Must Hurt a Lot.* Multnomah, 1988.
Preschoolers
Describes a boy's reaction of anger, grief, and eventual acceptance when his dog dies.

Varley, Susan. *Badger's Parting Gifts.* HarperTrophy, 1992.
Preschoolers
Badger's friends are sad when he dies but treasure the memories he left them.

Viorst, Susan. *The Tenth Good Thing about Barney.* Aladdin Library, 1987.
Preschoolers
A boy tries to think of the ten best things about his dead cat.

Wilhelm, Hans. *I'll Always Love You.* Dragonfly, 1988.
Preschoolers
A child's family grieves the death of their beloved dachshund, Elfie.

Death of a Loved One

Aliki. *The Two of Them.* William Morrow, 1987.
Preschoolers
Describes a little girl's relationship with her grandfather until his death.

Bibliography

Bryant-Mole, Karen. *Talking about Death.* Raintree/Steck Vaughn, 1999.
Preschoolers
Focuses on death as part of a natural life cycle.

Bunting, Eve. *The Big Red Barn.* Harcourt, 1979.
Preschoolers
A barn burning and the death of her mother threaten a youngster's sense of security.

________. *Happy Funeral.* Harpercollins Juvenile Books, 1982.
Preschoolers
A Chinese-American girl assists in the preparations for her grandfather's funeral.

________. *Rudi's Pond.* Houghton Mifflin, 1999.
Preschoolers
When a sick boy dies, his classmates remember him by building a school pond.

Buscaglia, Leo. *The Fall of Freddie the Leaf.* Henry Holt, 2002.
Preschoolers
As Freddie experiences the changing seasons, he learns that death is part of life.

Carson, Jo. *You Hold Me and I'll Hold You.* Orchard Books, 1992.
Toddlers and preschoolers
A girl finds comfort in being held at her great aunt's funeral.

Clifton, Lucille. *Everett Anderson's Goodbye.* Bt Bound, 1999.
Preschoolers
Everett copes with and accepts the fact of his father's death.

Cohn, Janice D.S.W. *I Had a Friend Named Peter.* William Morrow, 1987.
Preschoolers
Betsy's parents and teacher answer her questions after the death of her friend.

Cooke, Trish. *The Grandad Tree.* Candlewick Press, 2000.
Preschoolers
Their apple tree reminds two children of their dead grandfather.

DePaola, Tomie. *Nana Upstairs and Nana Downstairs.* Puffin, 2000.
Preschoolers
Four-year-old Tommy learns to face the reality of death.

Fraustino, Lisa Rowe. *The Hickory Chair.* Arthur A. Levine, 2001.
Preschoolers
A blind boy tells of the gift his grandmother left him after her death.

Heegaard, Marge E. *When Someone Very Special Dies.* Woodland Press, 1988.
Preschoolers
A practical format that helps children understand the concept of death and how to cope.

Hines, Anna Grossnickle. *Remember the Butterflies.* Dutton Books, 1991.
Preschoolers
After Grandpa dies, two children remember the special times they had with him.

Johnson, Joy, Merv Johnson, and Marvin Johnson. *Where's Jess?* Centering Corporation, 1982.
Preschoolers
A small boy learns what death is about when he notices that his sibling is gone.

Joosse, Barbara M. *Ghost Wings.* Chronicle Books, 2001.
Preschoolers
The monarch butterflies symbolize a Mexican girl's grief over her grandmother's death.

Krasny, Laurie and Marc Brown. *When Dinosaurs Die.* Little Brown & Co., 1998.
Toddlers and preschoolers
How people may feel about the death of loved ones and ways to honor their memory.

Miles, Miska. *Annie and the Old One.* Little Brown & Co., 1972.
Preschoolers
A Navajo girl believes that finishing weaving a rug means the death of her grandmother.

Mellonie, Bryan, and Robert Ingpen. *Lifetimes.* Hill of Content Publishing Co., 1983.
Schweibert, Pat, and Chuck De Klyen, Tear Soup. Perinatal Loss, 2001.
All ages.
A wonderfully illustrated book about how all of us grieve loss in our lives.

Sgouros, Charissa. *A Pillow for My Mom.* Houghton Mifflin/Walter Lorraine Books, 1998.
Preschoolers
A girl makes a pillow for her mom to make her more comfortable before she dies.

Thomas, Jane Resh. *Saying Good-Bye to Grandma.* Clarion Books, 1988.
Preschoolers
Susie wonders what Grandma's funeral will be like.

Winsch, Jane Loretta. *After the Funeral.* Paulist Press, 1995.
Preschoolers
Discusses the feelings that accompany the death of a loved one.

Zolotow, Charlotte. *My Grandson Lew.* Harpercollins Juvenile Books, 2004.
Preschoolers
Lew and his mother remember Grandpa together.

DIVORCE

Baum, Lois. *One More Time.* Mulberry Books, 1992.
Preschoolers
Shows the everyday life of a divorced father and his young son.

Boegehold, Betty. *Daddy Doesn't Live Here Anymore.* Golden Books, 1985.
Toddlers and preschoolers
Casey's thinks her parents' divorce is her fault and plans to get them back together.

Bunting, Eve. *The Days of Summer.* Harcourt, 2001.
Preschoolers.
Two girls try to deal with the news that their grandparents are getting a divorce.

Girard, Linda Walvoord. *At Daddy's on Saturday.* Albert Whitman & Co., 1987.
Preschoolers
Katie keeps a loving relationship with her father even though he lives apart from her.

Heegard, Marge Eaton. *When Mom and Dad Separate.* Woodland Press, 1992.
Preschoolers
A workbook to help children deal with their feelings about separation and divorce.

Hopkins, Beverly H. *Changes: My Family and Me.* Child Welfare League of America, 1999
Preschoolers
A basic explanation of the changes a family may go through after parents divorce.

Impey, Rose. *My Mom and Our Dad.* Viking, 1991.
Toddlers and preschoolers
Describes the feelings common to children who experience separation and divorce.

Krasny, Laurie, and Marc Brown. *Dinosaurs Divorce.* Little, Brown & Co., 1985.
Preschoolers
Describes the range of feelings divorce produces for youngsters.

Lansky, Vicky. *It's Not Your Fault, Koko Bear.* Book Peddlers, 2003.
Preschoolers
A read-together book for parents and young children during divorce.

Lindsay, Jeanne Warren. *Do I Have a Daddy?* Morning Glory Press, 2000.
Preschoolers
A single mother explains to her son that his daddy left soon after he was born.

Nightingale, Lois V. *My Parents Still Love Me Even though They're Getting a Divorce.* Nightingale Rose Publications, 1997.
Preschoolers
An interactive tale and tips for divorcing couples with children.

Robin, Prince Monroe. *Why Don't We Live Together Anymore?* Concordia Publishing House, 1998.
Preschoolers
Talks about changes in finances, moving, and visitation.

Disasters

Anderson, John Lonzo. *The Day the Hurricane Happened.* Atheneum, 1974.
Preschoolers
A family experiences the drama, danger, and destruction of a hurricane.

Enderle, Judith A. *Francis, the Earthquake Dog.* Chronicle Books, 1996.
Preschoolers
A story about the 1906 San Francisco earthquake and of a dog found in the rubble.

Fleischman, Paul. *Lost! A Story in String.* Henry Holt, 1999.
Preschoolers
A young girl uses her wits to survive when she's lost in the snow.

Givon, Hannah Gelman. *We Shake in a Quake.* Tricycle Press,1996.
Preschoolers
Captures a boys experience during an earthquake and tells how to prepare for one.

Harshman, Marc. *The Storm.* Cobblehill, 1995.
Preschoolers
Though confined to a wheelchair, Jonathan acts heroically before a tornado.

Shannon, David. *The Rain Came Down.* Blue Sky Press, 2000.
Toddlers and preschoolers
Captures the chaos that accompanies an unexpected downpour.

Szilagyi, Mary. *Thunderstorm.* Atheneum, 1985.
Preschoolers
Mother comforts her daughter and the daughter comforts her dog during a storm.

White, Linda Arms. *Comes a Wind.* DK Publishing, 2000.
Preschoolers
Two brothers swap tales abut the fiercest wind they had ever seen.

Wiesner, David. *Hurricane.* Clarion Books, 1990.
Preschoolers
The morning after a hurricane a broken tree becomes a magical place of adventure.

Zolotow, Charlotte. *The Storm Book.* HarperTrophy, 1989.
Preschoolers
A summer storm sweeps over the town and countryside.

Other Books on Related Topics

Girard, Linda Walvoord. *My Body Is Private*. Albert Whitman & Co., 1986.
Toddlers and preschoolers
Introduces the topic of sexual abuse and ways to keep one's body private.

McKinley, Robin. *My Father Is in the Navy*. Greenwillow, 1992.
Preschoolers
Sara hears that her father is coming home from the navy, but she doesn't remember him.

Martin, Chia. *We Like to Nurse*. Hohm Press, 1994.
Babies–preschoolers
A sweet book to read at bedtime before nursing.

Morgan, Stacy Towle. *The Cuddlers*. La Leche League International, 1993.
Toddlers and preschoolers
Describes the beauty of cuddling.

Moutoussamy-Ashe, Jeanne. *Daddy and Me*. Alfred A. Knopf, 1993.
Preschoolers
Life-affirming value for children dealing with long-term illness of a parent.

Numeroff, Laura, Wendy S. Harpham, and David M. McPhail. *The Hope Tree*. Simon & Schuster, 2001.
Preschoolers
A comforting picture book written to help children cope with a mother's breast cancer.

Pinczuk, Jane M. *Michele: The Nursing Toddler—A Story about Sharing Love*. La Leche League International, 1998.
Toddlers and preschoolers
With mother's milk and her family's love, Michele blooms from an infant to a toddler.

Spelman, Cornelia Maude. *Your Body Belongs to You.* Albert Whitman & Co., 2000.
Preschoolers
Helps parents talk to their young children about good and bad touching.

Stadler, John. *What's So Scary?* Orchard Books, 2001.
Toddlers and preschoolers
An illustrator draws animals for a book to figure out where they really belong.

Books for Parents and Caregivers

Acredolo, Linda, and Susan Goodwyn. *Baby Signs: How to Talk with Your Baby before Your Baby Can Talk.* McGraw-Hill/Contemporary Books, 2002.
This updated classic shows you how to encourage your baby's use of nonverbal gestures to enhance communication.

Bevere, Lisa. *Be Angry [But Don't Blow It]: Maintaining Your Passion without Losing Your Cool.* Thomas Nelson, 2000.
Teaches readers how to channel passionate emotions constructively.

Bolton, Iris. *My Son...My Son: A Guide to Healing after a Suicide in the Family.* Bolton Press Atlanta, 1983.
Provides resources, lists steps to take, and shows how to give comfort in the aftermath of a suicide.

Brazelton, T. Berry. *Touchpoints: Your Child's Emotional and Behavioral Development, Birth–3: The Essential Reference for the Early Years.* Perseus Press, 1992.
Treats problems that accompany the turning points in a child's development during the first years of life.

Canfield, Ken R. *The 7 Secrets of Effective Fathers: Becoming the Father You Want to Be.* Tyndale, 1995.
Draws on profiles of over five thousand fathers nationwide to help fathers to strengthen their family roles.

Cart, Michael. *911: The Book of Help.* Cricket Books, 2002.
Award-winning writers share their responses to the September 11, 2001 tragedy.

Cline, Foster W., and Jim Fay. *Parenting with Love and Logic: Teaching Children Responsibility.* Navpress, 1990.
Helps parents teach their children responsibility and coping skills by solving their own problems within the context of a healthy, loving relationship.

Cloud, Dr. Henry, and Dr. John Townsend. *Boundaries with Kids: When to Say Yes, When to Say No, to Help Your Children Gain Control of Their Lives.* Zondervan, 2001.
Helps parents set boundaries with their children.

Coleman, William L. *What Children Need to Know When Parents Get Divorced.* Bethany House, 1998.
Discusses the causes and results of divorce, emphasizing the needs of children.

Coloroso, Barbara. *Parenting through Crisis: Helping Kids in Times of Loss, Grief, and Change.* HarperResource, 2000.
Concrete, compassionate ideas for supporting children as they develop their own constructive ways of responding to life's challenges.

DeFoore, William Gray. *Anger: Deal with It, Heal with It, Stop It from Killing You.* Health Communications, 1991.
Helps link anger to its source and shows how to acknowledge, express, and manage it in a healthy manner.

Dentemaro, Christine, and Rachel Kranz. *Straight Talk about Anger.* Facts on File Inc., 1995.
Discusses biological reasons for anger, presents strategies for releasing it constructively, and gives suggestions for using it as an ally to correct injustice.

Emswiler, Mary Ann, and James P. Emswiler. *Guiding Your Child through Grief.* Bantam, 2000.
Down-to-earth handbook for dealing with the initial shock of death to identifying typical reactions by age group and achieving the main goals of family grieving.

Fitzgerald, Helen. *The Grieving Child: A Parent's Guide.* Fireside, 1992.
A guide for parents seeking to explain the death of a parent, relative, friend, or even a pet to a child.

Ford, Judy. *Wonderful Ways to Love a Child.* Fine Communications, 1997.
A down-to-earth guide for parents who want to put love into action and give their children the very best start in life.

Fraiberg, Selma H. *The Magic Years: Understanding and Handling the Problems of Early Childhood.* Scribner, 1996.
This reissued classic takes the reader into the mind of a child, showing how he confronts the world and learns to cope with it.

Garcia, W. Joseph. *Sign with Your Baby.* Northlight Communications, 2002.
How to communicate with children before they can speak.

Goldman, Linda. *Life and Loss: A Guide to Help Grieving Children.* Brunner-Routledge, 1999.
Teaches readers to recognize and understand different types of childhood losses while avoiding the clichés that block feeling.

Goleman, Daniel. *Emotional Intelligence.* Bantam, 1997.
Defines emotional intelligence in terms of self-awareness, altruism, personal motivation, empathy, and the ability to love and be loved by friends, partners, and family members.

Gottman, John M. *Raising an Emotionally Intelligent Child.* Simon & Schuster, 1998.
Provides a series of exercises to assess parenting styles and emotional self-awareness and identifies an "emotion coaching"

process to help teach children how to recognize and address their feelings.

Greene, Ross W. *The Explosive Child: A New Approach for Understanding and Parenting Easily Frustrated, Chronically Inflexible Children.* HarperCollins, 2001.
Equips parents with the skills needed to prevent or defuse the intense situations that can occur with a volatile child.

Greenspan, Stanley I., MD, and Nancy Thorndike Greenspan. *First Feelings: Milestones in the Emotional Development of Your Baby and Child.* Penguin, 1994
Emphasizes parental interaction as the key to a child's healthy, emotional maturation.

Hogg, Tracy, with Melinda Blau. *Secrets of the Baby Whisperer: How to Calm, Connect, and Communicate with Your Baby.* Ballantine Books, 2002.
Focusing on newborns and their parents, this volume teaches parents how to decipher their infant's cries, gestures, and facial expressions.

________. *Secrets of the Baby Whisperer for Toddlers.* Ballantine Books, 2002.
This volume introduces specific tools for engaging and managing toddlers.

Huggins, Kathleen, Harriette Hartigan, and Ruth A. Lawrence. *The Nursing Mother's Companion.* National Book Network, 1999.
Intended as a practical manual, this book combines specific advice with frequent, clear, and informative illustrations.

James, John W., and Russell Friedman. *When Children Grieve: For Adults to Help Children Deal with Death, Divorce, Pet Loss, Moving, and Other Losses.* HarperCollins, 2001.
A cutting-edge volume to free children from the false idea of "not feeling bad" and to empower them with positive, effective methods of dealing with loss.

Jarratt, Claudia Jewett. *Helping Children Cope with Separation and Loss*. Harvard Common Press, 1994.
Deals with divorce, death, absence, adoption, and foster care.

Karen, Robert, PhD. *Becoming Attached: First Relationships and How They Shape Our Capacity to Love*. Oxford Press, 1998.
What attachment theory has to tell us about the importance of early relationships.

Kübler-Ross, Elisabeth. *On Children and Death*. Scribner, 1997.
Based on a decade of working with dying children, the author of this compassionate book offers the families of dead and dying children the help and hope they need to survive.

________. *On Death and Dying*. Scribner, 1997.
Gives the reader a better understanding of how imminent death affects a patient, the professionals who serve that patient, and the patient's family, bringing hope to all involved.

Leach, Penelope. *Your Baby and Child: from Birth to Age Five*. Alfred A. Knopf, 1989.
Describes what is happening to your child, what he or she is doing, experiencing, and feeling, at different stages from birth through starting school.

Lynch-Fraser, Diane. *Life's Little Miseries: Helping Your Child with the Disasters of Everyday Life*. Rowman & Littlefield, 1992.
A parents' guide to handling the everyday concerns of children aged three to twelve, whether it's dealing with nightmares, starting school, or moving to a new house.

MacDonald, Margaret Read. *The Parent's Guide to Storytelling*. Little Folk, 2001.
How to make up stories and retell old favorites.

McClure, Vimala Schneider. *Infant Massage: A Handbook for Loving Parents*. Bantam Books, 2000.
Helps you master the techniques of infant massage so you can incorporate this healing art into your baby's life.

Miller, Susan. *After the Boxes Are Unpacked: Moving on after Moving In*. Focus on the Family, 1998.
Insight, inspiration, and encouragement for coping with the losses and grief that moving can bring.

Ramey, Craig T., and Sharon L. Ramey. *Right from Birth: Building Your Child's Foundation for Life (Birth to 18 Months)*. Goddard Press, 1999.
What counts and what works in raising good-natured, capable, confident, caring, and accomplished children right from birth.

Sanger, Sirgay, MD. *Baby Talk, Parent Talk: Understanding Your Baby's Body Language*. Doubleday, 1990.
Discusses the wide variety of emotions children experience, including disgust, fear, sadness, contentment, joy, surprise, and even the desire to be left alone.

Sears, William. *Creative Parenting: How to Use the Attachment Parenting Concept to Raise Children Successfully from Birth through Adolescence*. Dodd Mead, 1987.
A reference book written in an interesting and practical style that covers every developmental stage.

Seeger, Pete, and Paul Dubois Jacobs. *Peter Seeger's Storytelling Book*. Harcourt, 2000.
A valuable resource for storytellers from one of America's most beloved musicians.

Tatelbaum, Judy. *The Courage to Grieve: Creative Living, Recovery and Growth through Grief*. Perennial, 1984.
Offers readers comfort and provides the specific help they need to face their grief fully and to recover and grow from the experience.

Thoman, Evelyn B., and Sue Browder. *Born Dancing: How Intuitive Parents Understand Their Baby's Unspoken Language and Natural Rhythm*. HarperCollins, 1987.
Emphasizes how parental awareness of and response to a baby's internal rhythms establish trust.

Viorst, Judith. *Necessary Losses: The Loves, Illusions, Dependencies, and Impossible Expectations That All of Us Have to Give Up in Order to Grow.* Free Press, 1998.
How we grow and change through the losses that are an inevitable and necessary part of life.

Wallerstein, Judith S., and Joan Berlin Kelly. *Surviving the Breakup: How Children and Parents Cope with Divorce.* Basic Books, 1996.
The adjustment of a child of divorced parents depends more on what happens after the divorce than on conditions in the predivorce family.

Wallerstein, Judith S., and Sandra Blakeslee. *Second Chances: Men, Women and Children a Decade after Divorce, Who Wins, Who Loses, and Why.* Mariner Books, 1996.
A look at the child's perspective on the loss of the intact family unit.

Wallerstein, Judith S., Julia M. Lewis, and Sandra Blakeslee. *The Unexpected Legacy of Divorce: The Twenty-Five Year Landmark Study.* Hyperion, 2001.
Divorce takes its greatest toll on the children of divorce when they reach adulthood and embark on romantic relationships of their own.

Whitehouse, Elaine, and Warwick Pudney. *A Volcano in My Tummy: Helping Children to Handle Anger.* New Society Publishers, 1996.
A resource book for parents, caregivers, and teachers.

Wolfelt, Alan D., PhD. *A Child's View of Grief.* Center for Loss and Life Transition, 1991.
This concise resource for parents of grieving kids explores several key principles for helping children cope with grief and offers ways to create an emotional environment filled with love and acceptance.

________. *Healing Your Grieving Heart for Kids: 100 Practical Ideas.* Companion Press, 2001.

Offers suggestions, simple advice, and activities for healing activities that can help children learn to express their grief and mourn naturally after a death.

________. *Helping Children Cope with Grief.* Accelerated Development, 1983.
Presents techniques for creating an atmosphere in which a grieving child can thrive, including a chapter on empathic understanding.

Wurman, Richard Saul. *Understanding Children.* TOP, 2002.
A guidebook covering a wide range of topics for anyone who takes care of young children.